MW00528510

Dear Aunt Gail,

Thank you for reading this book and keeping their memories and sacrifices alive.

Your Loving Nephew

Michael Hubert

LEAVING CAMPUS

A WORLD WAR II EPITAPH

The Account of the Students of Bemidji State
Teachers College Who Left College Life in World War II
to Serve in the Military and Died in Service

DR. MICHAEL HERBERT

Fulton Books, Inc.
Meadville, PA

Published by Fulton Books 2022

ISBN 978-1-63985-695-4 (paperback)
ISBN 978-1-63985-736-4 (hardcover)
ISBN 978-1-63985-696-1 (digital)

Printed in the United States of America

To all of those who served, both overseas and on the home front, military and civilian, in helping to defeat the powers of fascism in World War II.

Banner Posted on the Centennial Quad, Bemidji
State University. 2019. (Photo by Author)

We leave you our deaths.
Give them their meaning.
We were young, they say.
We have died; remember us.

(Archibald MacLeish 1982–1982)

ACKNOWLEDGMENTS

John Swartz
Colleen Deel
Eloise Graves-Jallin
Pat Beaumont
Bob McPartlin
Deborah Herbert
Michael J. Herbert
Mallary Herbert

PROLOGUE

LET THIS BOOK SERVE AS a memorial and tribute to all of those who have died in the service to their country during World War II. Let us not forget the sacrifices made by those brave men and women. May we all be citizens worth fighting, and even dying for. To the best of my ability, I have accomplished due diligence in the research accumulated. I have spent the last twenty-one months constructing this work. Unfortunately, due to the passing of the decades, records, photographs, relatives, and other forms of remembrance have been lost to time.

1941

The 1941 fall season in northern Minnesota marked an exciting time for the new and returning students of the Bemidji State Teacher's College. This was the college's twenty-second year as an institution and while the college was experiencing an enrollment drop of 23 percent as compared to the previous fall, it was also proud of having all two- and four-year graduates of the class of 1941 placed in positions, the vast majority in education. The fall class of students numbered 375, with 145 of those students being freshmen.

Freshman Registration 1941. (Bemidji State University Library Archives)

The news of plans for Homecoming activities and the first Pepfest was fresh on the student's minds. There were now plans for a new library and word that faculty member Dr. A. C. Clark had received his PhD. Students such as *Johnnie Shock* were back to serve in many student roles, such as the co-editor of the student paper, th*e Northern Student."*

The "B" club held its first meeting on September 30, with *Jack McCormick* elected as this year's president and *Johnnie Shock* as treasurer.

While at that time, most students were aware of the war going on in Europe, with Hitler invading Poland in 1938 and the Japanese invasion of China and Manchuria in 1937, little did they anticipate the world events which would drag the United States into a world war. In just a few short months, the surprise attack by the Japanese Naval forces on the American forces at Pearl Harbor, Hawaii, would drastically change the lives of all of those at the college, in both small relatively inconsequential ways to, by wars end, having lost the lives of twenty current students.

September marked the announcement of several "colorful" assemblies, ranging from class meetings in preparation for Homecoming to singers and a physical education show. It was also announced that there were six new faculty members added to the college staff.

October of 1941 was marked with the opening of the football season, the selection of the Homecoming royalty and a week of various Homecoming events, which included a parade, dance and bonfire. There was an alumni luncheon planned for the day of the Homecoming game along with a post-game party. The official kick-off of Homecoming was held at the fairgrounds on Friday evening, October 3, with the crowning of the Homecoming Queen and introduction of the football team. This was followed by a snake dance through downtown Bemidji and a Victrola dance held in the gymnasium. The Homecoming football game was won by the Beavers over Winona Warriors by a score of 13–0 Saturday evening. The first Beaver touchdown was scored in the second half by *Jack McCormick*, who also converted the place kick.

Many other typical college organizations and activities went on as normal but were soon to be dramatically changed due to the war. The shortage of male students due to enlistment would reduce if not eliminate many of the activity's students looked forward to.

1941 Bemidji State Teachers College Acapella
Choir. (Bemidji State University Archives)

1941 Bemidji State Teachers College League of Women
Voters. (Bemidji State University Archives)

1941 Women's Athletic Association. (Bemidji State University Archives)

Team sports decreased from the years starting in 1942 through 1945 due to the lack of available male students. In addition to the traditional sports (almost exclusively restricted to male students) there were intramural sports as well.

1942 Men's Track Team. (Bemidji State University Archives)

1940s Intramural Curling. (Bemidji State University Archives)

1941 BSTC Homecoming Court October 3, 4, and 5. June Sellberg, Queen Wanda Worth, Rachel Peterson, Dorothy Setterholm, Paula Bruss, and Jean Hatch. (Bemidji State University Archives)

The Rural Life club held a "Tramp Hike" to Diamond Point Park on October 14 and the Sketch club had already made plans to start making Christmas cards for sale to students and faculty members. The club also will be decorating certain school windows for Christmas.

Archery class was underway in October with sixteen students. The student with the high score using thirty arrows at forty yards was *Jim Lizer*. The class will later move out to sixty- and seventy-yard targets. The class is for students who are majoring in physical education as well as students who are simply interested in archery for recreation.

Other noteworthy news that fall quarter at BSTC was the announcement that six students had been named to the 1941 edition of *Who's Who in American Colleges and Universities*.[1] One of the six named students was *John Shock*.

Reading left to right: Paula Bruss, Herbert Fisher, Dorothy Setterholm, John Shock, Rachel Peterson and Wade Davis.

John Shock, fourth from the left. *The Northern Student*, November 28, 1941. (Bemidji State University Archives)

November marked the coming of the winter season. The college observed education week by introduced by an assembly which included the history of education week, readings, and music provided by the A Cappella choir and Glee club. Dr. Sattgast, president of the college, gave a talk entitled, "The Present Emergency and Bemidji State Teachers College." The aim of education week is, by education, to banish illiteracy, physical unfitness, and public misinformation. November also noted the selection by the coaches of the Minnesota State Teachers colleges of *Jack McCormick*, who is in his third year

[1] Randall H. Pettus, ed., *Who's Who. The Official Who's Who Among Students in American Universities and Colleges. Volume VIII. 1941–1942,* (Tuscaloosa, Alabama: Randall Publishing Company, 1942).

as running back, as honorary captain of the Teachers Colleges All-Stars football team. That month also marked the near completion of the fourth class of the Civil Aeronautics Authority (CAA) pilots training school. Once students have completed this program, they are eligible to apply for their private pilot's license. Among those students listed in the class were *Kenneth Gregg* and *Roger Hilstad*. *John Shock*, along with four other members of the *Northern Student* staff attended the seventh annual Minnesota College Press convention at St. Cloud Teachers College. The dramatics program presented two one-act plays at an assembly program on November 28. Members of the cast of Arthur Hopkin's comedy *Moonshiners* were Bjarne Stengel and *Roger Hilstad*. On a more negative note, this year's Thanksgiving party (one considered by many to be one of the bigger parties held each year) was canceled due to reduced enrollment and the resulting drop in the activity fund that would have paid for the party. However, it was suggested that more Victrola dances on free Friday evenings would help lessen the loss of the Thanksgiving party. One student wished to know why BSTC did not have a Sadie Hawkins dance when other colleges held them. Various music groups and soloists were performing off campus, which included BSTC students performing at the Northwest Singers Annual Concert held in Bagley on Sunday, November 16. Among those performing was the clarinet quintet consisting of Harry Stoner, *Walter Brotherton*, Irene Torgerson, Ted Moleski, and Byron Graves.

It was noted that one out of every incoming freshman was either a valedictorian or salutatorian in their high school graduating class. Included in that list was *Charles Marmorine*.

Returning to the basketball team was all-conference guard *Jack McCormick*, who had just ended his senior year on the football team, as it also ended for *John Shock*, both having earned the letter in football at the end of the season.

With the surprise attack by the Japanese naval and air forces on Pearl Harbor on December 7, 1941, came a dramatic realization that life would be very different for everyone, including the students, faculty, and staff at Bemidji State Teachers College. There were many forums and discussions held on campus conducted by faculty and students alike. At one such panel discussion, Dr. Sattgast made mention that the student who chooses to remain in college instead of enlisting is not a "slacker" and pointed out that college-trained people are more able to readjust and rehabilitate a country to the changed conditions that exist after the war.

December of 1941 marked the installment of the first tunnels at BSTC, that which will run between Deputy Hall and the gymnasium. The A Cappella choir had set their Christmas concert for December 14 at the First Lutheran Church. The students proposed a trial "blackout" at the annual Christmas party as a national defense measure. Winter social events were scheduled, which included a midwinter party to be held on February 13, sponsored by the rural life club as well as a number of college Victrola dancing parties, which were very popular.

On a more serious note, special training courses were now being offered as a direct result of the United States being at war. First aid, laboratory techniques, and international radio code were three of the courses brought into the curriculum as they were seen as being valuable to boys who would be going into training as well as girls who may be asked to serve. Male students who were enrolled in aviation were informed that the radio code course was now mandatory, as it was reported that the army and maritime services had a shortage of radio operators. The laboratory course was designed to be especially helpful to any boys entering the medical corps.

The possibility of war had been on students' minds for several years then, and in December of 1939, the student paper, *The Northern Student*, conducted a poll of students at the BSTC regarding possible involvement by the United States in a world war. When asked, "Do you favor strict US Neutrality?" 84 percent of respondents replied yes. That same percentage (84 percent) felt that the United States could stay out of war while 94 percent of respondents felt that there was no danger of the United States being invaded in the near future.[2]

---

[2] Unaccredited, *Northern Student*, December 2, 1939, 2.

January marked the first meeting of the BSTC Playmakers Club, a drama club of whom *Roger Hilstad* was a charter member. The Playmakers planned to present *The Late Christopher Bean*.

The cast of *The Late Christopher Bean*. *Roger Hilstad*, third standing from the left. *Northern Student*, Wednesday, January 28, 1942, p. 3. (Bemidji State University Archives)

Due to the war, there was increasing demand for teachers. Due to the war emergency, the six Minnesota State Teachers colleges enacted temporary changes in curriculum as long as the war was ongoing. These changes included, by including summer courses, students could graduate from the four-year program by attending only ten quarters, instead of the current twelve, and a one-year course for rural teachers was also approved.

Defense stamps were now being offered on sale every Tuesday in the halls of the laboratory school, and there was an ongoing promotion for students to start a savings account in order to help Uncle Sam. While there was a decided shift in college life due to the war, the students also tried to maintain a sense of normalcy. The all-college costume ball was scheduled for February 12 and sponsored by the Rural Life club. All that was required by the students was "his activity ticket, a disguised appearance, and an unquestioning frame of mind." (*Northern Student*, 1942)

Jack McCormick ended his outstanding athletic career at the end of the '41–'42 basketball season by enlisting in the US Army Air Corps. Jack was regarded as one of the best all-around athletes in BSTC history. Jack was under consideration for "big-time professional" football before enlisting. While at BSTC Jack majored in physical education and social studies.

Jack McCormick. *The Northern Student*, Friday, January 26, 1940, p. 4. (Bemidji State University Archives)

1942

At the January 12, 1942, meeting of the "B" club, *Johnny Shock* was elected as club president. Topics such as "Adjusting Women to Their Jobs" were held on campus, and it was spoken that women in England were recognized as equals with the men and were working in uniform. An interesting note was that English women of higher class were not accustomed to filling positions of unskilled and untrained workers, which reportedly, were performed willingly. Continued changes in curriculum brought into place to meet the college war emergency program were explained by President Sattgast to the student body in January. Some of those changes included were the elimination of Easter vacation except for Good Friday and Easter Monday; the college would close a week earlier than usual; and the study into the possibility of running two sessions concurrently. Freshmen who were at least eighteen and had completed twenty-two quarter hours would be now able to apply for aviation training under the Civilian Pilot Training (CPT) program.

It was noted in the student paper that former student, *Edgar Arnold*, who was at BSTC in 1941, was now in the Air Corps training program at the naval station at Corpus Christi, Texas. He expects to finish his training sometime in March and hoped to visit before going on active duty. "He writes nonchalantly of flying a grandpa seagull that weighs twelve ton and has a wingspread of one hundred four feet. And here we set—!"[3]

There existed an ongoing discussion regarding the lack of male students due to the war, and how the female students felt about that. One female student wrote in an article that "it is true that girls are

---

[3] Edgar Arnold, *Northern Student*, Vol. XV (February 1942), 2.

'sighing in gusty boredom' and are 'wandering dispiritedly about the halls of the institution.' But it is very possible and probable that it isn't because the war has taken all of our 'reasonably presentable males.'"[4]

Students were encouraged through the student paper under the article, "Dear Soldier," to write to their fellow students who were now a member of the armed forces. One of those former students was Air Cadet *Edgar P. Arnold*, who, as of February 1942 listed as being stationed at Bldg. 24-8, Room 241, Naval Air Station, Corpus Christi, Texas.

It was noted that in February of 1942, the students of the eighth-grade mathematics class sold defense stamps and bonds to the students of the college and those in the laboratory school. It was reported that as of the twenty-fifth of the month the eighth graders had sold $245 worth of stamps and bonds.

Elementary School Laboratory School Students Purchasing Defense Stamps. *The Northern Student*, February 25, 1942, p. 2. (Bemidji State University Archives)

---

[4] Anonymous, *Northern Student*, Vol. XV (February 1942).

It was an exciting time for Beaver basketball as their victory 38–36 over the Mankato Teachers College Indians won the Beavers the championship for the third time in three years of the Northern Teachers Athletic Conference.

In June of 1942, athletic awards were given out, including football jackets to *John Shock, Jack McCormick*, and *Jim Lizer*.

As demands for military recruits increased, Bemidji State was approved for programs under which men enrolled in those approved programs may enlist in the Army or Navy Air Corps Reserve immediately and complete their two or four years of college before being called for training.

May of 1942 marked the graduation of ninety Bemidji State students—thirty-four-year graduates and sixty-two-year graduates—which was held at the college gymnasium after the baccalaureate sermon, which was held at the Methodist church. President and Mrs. Sattgast held a buffet dinner for the seniors at their home on May 24.

June also noted that 1200 high school seniors attended the college's Guest Day. This day included a regional track meet and a luncheon for high school valedictorians and salutatorians given by the Alpha Phi Sigma. The day's activities also included tours of the college, the city of Bemidji, Lake Bemidji, as well as an afternoon concert by the A Cappella choir and band. The end of the day's activities was two one-act plays given by the Playmakers and a dance for guests from 5:00 p.m. to 8:00 p.m. A full day indeed!

In the Wednesday, June 3, 1942, edition of the *Northern Student*, it was noted that among those leaving for induction into the Army was *John Shock*.

John Shock. *Northern Student*, June 3, 1942, p.4.
(Bemidji State University Archives)

Robert McPartlin
Died in Service September 1, 1942

While Bemidji State was preparing for the start of the 1942–1943 academic year, tragedy first struck the student body.

Robert (Bob) J. McPartlin was the first Bemidji State Teachers College student to be killed in action on September 1, 1942. Robert was born on April 29, 1920, in International Falls, Minnesota, son of Mr. and Mrs. F. J. McPartlin. Robert attended grade school at St. Phillips school in Bemidji, Minnesota. After Robert completed grade school at St. Phillips, he attended Bemidji High School and graduated with his high school diploma in 1938.

Robert (Bob) McPartlin High School Photo.
(Courtesy of Robert McPartlin)

Robert then moved to the Twin Cities and attended two years of college at the University of Minnesota and then came back to Bemidji and attended Bemidji State Teachers College to finish up courses that were required for Robert to be eligible for aviation training with the Army Air Corps. Robert enrolled at the Bemidji State Teachers College the fall quarter of 1940.

In the spring of 1941, Robert went to Cuero Field, Texas to apply for pilot training. Cuero Field was an Army Air Corps Airfield training facility located at the Cuero municipal airfield, which was located two miles west of the town of Cuero, Texas. At Cuero Field, all of the instructors and mechanics were civilians, but the training was supervised by the Army. Cuero Field produced thousands of pilots who served in the Army Air Corps during WWII.

Cuero Field, Texas during WWII. (Negative 099-0753, General Photograph Collection, USTA Special Collections)

Robert was not initially accepted when he applied for admittance in the spring of 1940 but was asked to reapply for either a bombardier or navigator position once Cuero Field had been ready to accept candidates for those positions.

Robert returned home for a short period of time and then moved to Los Angeles to work at the Lockheed factory until he was contacted by the Army Air Corps in the fall of 1941 for training as a navigator. Navigator training consisted of fifteen to twenty weeks of training at which time the navigator student learned precision dead-reckoning navigation with basic pilotage, radio operation, and celestial navigation. The navigation cadet logged approximately 100 hours in the air flying but for every hour of flight, he spent five hours in the classroom. In April of 1942, Robert graduated from Kelly Field, Texas, as a navigator. At that time, Robert was assigned various training missions at several locations throughout the country. At the end of July 1942, Robert and his crew were sent overseas from Essler Field, Louisiana.

From what letters were received by relatives told, Robert arrived in Egypt sometime around August 16, 1942.

Second Lieutenant Robert McPartlin. (Courtesy Robert McPartlin)

Robert was assigned as a navigator serving aboard the North American Aviation built B-25 "Mitchell" twin-engine bombers. The bombers were named "Mitchell" bombers after Brigadier General William "Billy" Mitchell. These bombers were very versatile and were used in a number of bombing roles. The B-25 was used for both high- and low-level bombing runs as well as antisubmarine patrol. The B-25 is most commonly remembered as the bomber that General Doolittle launched the first bombing raid against Japan on April 18, 1942, from the deck of the aircraft carrier Hornet.

B-25 Mitchell Bomber. (US Army Photograph)

Robert was assigned to the Eighty-Third Squadron, Twelfth Bomb Group (M), Ninth United States Army Air Force, which was attached to the British Eighth Army—based at Ismailia, Egypt—El Alamein. On September 14, it was reported in the *Bemidji Sentinel* that Robert had been reported missing since September 1. F. J. McPartlin, Robert's father had received the missing airman notice from the adjutant general's office in Washington, DC. It was sad to note that F. J. McPartlin had received a letter from Robert that same day dating from August 17. In that letter, Robert write, "not to worry about me if you get news about me that doesn't sound right," going on to explain that many reports that get out are not authentic. Robert was assigned as the navigator on a B-25 Mitchell and was completing his second bombing mission over El Alamein on September 1, 1942, targeting tanks, trucks, and enemy troops at the El Alamein front line. In his account of the flight, Staff Sergeant Roland Rakow, who was the radio operator and lower turret gunner, described what took place on their way back to the base after dropping their bomb load.

> On September 1, 1942, as our B-25 was return-
> ing from its second completed mission—drop-
> ping its bomb load on tanks, trucks, and troops
> on the front line at El Alamein—it was struck by

a German anti-aircraft 88 mm shell on the left side of the aircraft, adjacent to the top turret gun position. The shell made a gaping hole, which caused the aircraft to break open and go into a 30- or 40-degree dive. The bombardier, navigator, and the top turret gunner were unable to leave the aircraft. The pilot, co-pilot, and I (the radio operator) parachuted to the ground. We sustained wounds and injuries.

After the aircraft was hit, I looked for a way of escape and found the gaping hole where the shell had hit. After some effort, since the aircraft was in a dive, I bailed out at the hole. Before exiting, I looked for Sergeant Andersen. He should have been adjacent to the hole, as this was the location of the top turret gun. I could only conjecture that he had been blown out of the aircraft when the shell hit.

Jurine (the widow of 2nd Lt. Irving Biers, co-pilot of the plane) told me that although the plane had been hit by anti-aircraft fire, on its way down it had a mid-air collision with another Allied plane. The other plane was an A-20A South African bomber.

Roland had believed for nearly seventy years that enemy fire alone was involved in the crash.

"I was sitting right next to where that 88 mm shell came though the plane," he told Jurine. "And I jumped out of the hole it made."

"The pilots could not get out when the plane first started going down," Jurine told me. "They were held back in their seats by the centrifugal force, but after it hit a South African plane, their B-25 went into an inverted outside spin which pushed them forward."

They were then able to exit.

I bailed out and waited a few seconds, then felt for the ripcord—but I couldn't find it. Frantically, I tried to locate it and finally found it, almost completely behind my back.

With my last energy, I pulled the cord. The parachute opened with a jerk. My left arm became so entangled in the parachute's lines I sustained a compound fracture of the left clavicle. I had no control of the chute before hitting the ground, my face down. There was a strong wind as I landed. The parachute ballooned and dragged me approximately 300 feet, until German soldiers came and stopped me from being dragged farther.

Lt. Archer and Lt. McPartlin were unable to leave the aircraft and died in the crash. Capt. Croteau, Lt. Biers, and I parachuted to the ground. We landed in separate locations. Each of us sustained wounds and injuries.[5]

Within a short period of time, Capt. Croteau and Lt. Biers were each captured and subsequently transported to a German POW camp. They remained there for the duration of the war.

Dr. Stephen P. Johnson, a historian with the US Defense POW/Missing Personnel Office in Washington, DC, reported: "As you probably know, this agency [DPMO] tries to locate and identify the missing from past conflicts. My division responds to Congressional inquiries, and questions forwarded through the various service casualty offices. I'm researching such an inquiry at the time, and it con-

5   Roland Rankow, "Personal Interview with Dennis Hill," Camp 59 Survivors. June 9, 2013. https://camp59survivors.com/2013/06/09/roland-rakows-story-an-update/.

cerns S/Sgt Rakow's aircrew. The remains of McPartlin, Archer, and Anderson have never been recorded. The 83rd Bomb Squadron did not accomplish the required Missing Air Crew Report (MACR), and the unit records that did survive the war and make their way into the National Archives are sparse [fully understandable as they were busy fighting a war, but inconvenient for the historian trying to find the missing from the war]."[6]

(Courtesy of Bob McPartlin)

As could be expected, Roberts family was devastated by the news from the war department and there was a lengthy article in the *Bemidji Daily Pioneer* regarding Robert's death. At the conclusion of the article, Robert's father stated, "Our family is hard hit, as Bob was quite generally our family favorite. Of course, when one is gone, we always feel that he was the one we could least spare. But we know that Bob went as he wanted to go if he had to, fighting the good fight. His one dread in life was to be a cripple. The air service appealed to him because he said, 'If they shoot me down I'll be thru and not have to go through life a cripple.'"

Robert's mother wrote to the *Bemidji Daily Pioneer* and her letter was published in the Friday Evening of the paper on October 8, 1942.

---

[6] Steven P. Johnson, "Roland Rankow's Story—An Update (Interview)," US Defense POW/Missing Personnel Office, November 27, 2011.

Mrs. F. J. McPartlin, who with her husband, recently visited in Bemidji, has written from St. Paul that her son Robert who was killed in action with the United States air force had been awarded the Purple Heart medal. She writes that many of his friends may be interested in the account of some of his experiences after leaving training. Mrs. McPartlin writes: "Although Bob's plane was perhaps the first of the group to be shot down by the enemy their trip from camp in Louisiana to the Egyptian desert was full of thrills for them. They left camp July 17, 1942, to Tampa, Porto Rico and Brazil, picking up necessary equipment at each place—then across the Atlantic to Central Africa where they awaited orders. They went on to Cairo and the Holy Land in which they were most interested. His letter, which we determined from later information, was written from the Sudan country said, 'We know now we are not at any country club picnic.'

Bob's plane was shot down Sept. 1, 1942. Listening to an account over the radio of the drive in this territory we heard the report that 'only one plane did not return.'

Sept. 9, 1942, we were notified Bob was missing in action. In June this year the government notified us a grave was found on the desert and a cross with the words, 'Bombardier Archer and navigator' on it and also Bob's dog tag. The rest of the crew were taken prisoners and we have heard from them from a German prison.

Robert was posthumously awarded the Purple Heart and Air Medals.

According to the federal government Department of Defense POW/MIA Accounting agency, there are still 72,632 military service personnel not recovered following WWII. Of that 72,632, 1,402 were from Minnesota—Robert McPartlin being one of those missing.

US Military Museum, Carthage, Tunisia. (US AFRICOM Public Affairs, May 29, 2010)

* * * * *

With the start of the 1942–1943 academic year, there was a meeting held by a board of officers from the Army, Navy, and Marines, which was mandatory for all male students to explain up any misunderstandings surrounding the reserves enlistment program. All male students were excused from classes to attend these two-day meetings. The local newspaper, *The Bemidji Daily Pioneer*, noted on August 29, 1942, that the college had been approved by the Navy and war department to offer pre-officer training. Interested students could apply for this training, and if accepted, then enlists in the branch of service he chooses (Army or Navy) and can complete his degree prior to entering his chosen branch of the service. The students who choose this option would not receive any pay until they started active duty. Students enrolled in this program would have a curriculum that "emphasized physical training, mathematics, physics and military geography."[7] As students settled in for another fall semester, the various clubs and organizations started to become active. Enrollment for fall of 1942 had dropped significantly, as was not totally unexpected. Of the 253 students enrolled, 98 were men and 155 were women.

One of the first fall assemblies, held September 18, was titled "School and War Problems." A roundtable discussion was held in which it was discussed how the school was cooperating with the Army and Navy programs as well as information provided by the Victory Aides committee on ways civilians may aid the war program. Mr. John Glas explained the Civilian Pilots Training (CPT) course. The CPT trainee is an enlisted member of the Army Reserve Corps, and after the eight weeks of training at BSTC, they will be off for Hibbing or Fargo for advanced training, eventually going into the regular Army Air Corps.

The Rural Life club held its first meeting in September with guest speakers and the topic of discussion for that meeting being "Rural Youth's Responsibility Today and Tomorrow." At the Friday, September 25 assembly, an English movie, *Target for Tonight* was shown, which was a documentary showing an English bombing raid by British forces over Europe. The war was very much kept at the forefront of the student's minds. The shadow of war covered many of the activities typically held each year. The annual faculty formal dinner, which was held at the Markham hotel that fall, included a presentation by college President Sattgast entitled, "The College Professor's Responsibilities During Wartime." It was also announced that the college would be displaying a flag for servicemen which was six feet by nine feet in size, bearing a star for each student and faculty member who had entered the service since the registration of November 1940. At that time, there were 225 stars on the flag that was ordered. The

[7] Uncredited, "College Approved for Pre-Officer Training," *The Bemidji Daily Pioneer* (August 29, 1942), 2.

34

flag was ordered by President Sattgast and letters were sent out to the parents of those servicemen to ascertain the desired information.

Student Helen Perry wrote an article, "To the Boys in Service," for the *Northern Student* which typifies the thoughts of the student body regarding the war.

> So you're wondering what BSTC will be like this year? Will it be the same as when you left it? But why? Shouldn't it be expected that two successive years would be very similar? In other eras no doubt they would. But this, as we all know, is a time of struggle—a struggle for many things. And with this struggle have gone many of our youth—boys and girls alike. Girls have gone to work in places left vacant by men entering the service. And marching and training in the same ranks as those men are an innumerable number of you young men from this college. It is these vacancies, which we were vainly hoping would not be here, and which you knew would be, that are making you wonder what Bemidji will be like this year. Nor does it take long to find the answer to your questions. Faces in familiar places were immediately missed, and at the same time we experienced a hollow feeling inside of us. Did we give up hopes for a worthwhile year though? Naturally not. If we had, we would not be students of Bemidji State Teachers College. Of course it will not be the same; it couldn't be, but we are trying to carry out our duties here with a smile, and at the same time make new students feel that old friendly spirit which Bemidji is noted for and which we experienced. Nor are we forgetting you boys in service. Plans are springing up right and left for the purpose of keeping in

contact with you and for keeping you posted on BSTC activities.

So, even if it does make us feel soft inside to have to face these difficulties which are so noticeable, Bemidji Teachers college students are going to do their share towards keeping the institution the same friendly, sociable, and opportunity-laden college as the one that you boys left. And the inspiration for this will come from our contacts through correspondence and from our memories of you here—freshened by familiar activities in which you formerly participated.[8]

The annual formal dinner for the faculty was held at the Markham hotel on September 30. President C. R. Sattgast was the speaker for the evening, and his speech was entitled "The College Professor's Responsibilities During Wartime." The dinner was concluded with various social activities.

October of 1942 marked the start of Homecoming week's activities, which included a Pepfest, bonfire, twisting snake dance, and the selection of a Homecoming Queen to be concluded on Saturday with a parade, football game and dance.

---

[8] Helen Perry, "So You're Wondering What BSTC Will Be Like This Year," *Northern Student* (September 29, 1942).

Students Plan Homecoming

—Courtesy of Duluth Herald News Service

Busy in conference are the student members of the Homecoming committee. From left to right they are: LeRoy Clauson,
Doris Mix, Allen Higgins, coordinating chairman David Myerchin
and Priscilla Hepokoski.

The Northern Student, Tuesday, Sept. 29, 1942, p.
3. (Bemidji State University Archives)

The administration reported that overall college enrollment was down from 397 students the fall of 1941 to 253 students the fall of 1942. Of those 253 students, 38 percent were male students. President Sattgast noted that due to the war, the shortage could be expected, but once the war was over, he expected student enrollment to be around 500 students. The A Cappella choir began rehearsals, and the football team played its first game against Mankato Teachers college on October 2 and end up losing that game 7–0. *The Bemidji Daily Pioneer* noted the coming of the Homecoming week:

> A roaring bonfire, snappy Pepfest and twisting snake dance, a pretty new queen, a pretentious parade with an array of beautiful floats and a hard fought gridiron battle; these are the main attractions billed for the Bemidji State Teachers College Homecoming on October 8–11. Saturday is alumni day when the alumni will have a chance to renew old acquaintances and make new ones. On Saturday evening the alumni and students

are invited to attend the annual Homecoming dance in the college gym at 8:30 p.m.[9]

This year's Homecoming featured "Dads Day," whereupon the dads of the football teams' players would be invited to campus, be introduced at the Homecoming game and halftime and later that day would be guests at a banquet to be held at the Bemidji High School.

1942 Bemidji State Teachers College Football
Team. (Bemidji State University Archives)

The college was noticeably impacted by the war and caused may changes to be made to compensate for the lack of students. Mr. Thompson, the director of the A Capella Choir, noted that less than half of the choir members from last year had returned. Thompson reported that he was uncertain if there would be an opera that year as it would depend on the number of solo voices developed. Classes at the college were canceled on Tuesday, October 13 so students could help out with the scrap drive scheduled that day. As a result of the student's efforts, it was reported that the college had collected

[9]   Uncredited, "Homecoming Week," *The Bemidji Daily Pioneer* (October 2, 1942).

between thirty and thirty-five tons of scrap that day. That same day, sixty female students spent the day aiding the Red Cross by assisting in the making of surgical dressings. Other students from the college went out in cars with businessmen and acting as checkers and tabulators for the scrap collected.

1942 Homecoming Queen and Court. (Bemidji State University Library Archives)

Malcolm Getchell
Died in Service October 14, 1942

Sadly, on the same day as the scrap drive, the cost of war struck Bemidji State Teachers College a second time in two months with the reported death of *Malcolm Getchell*, who left BSTC to enlist in the Army Air Corps in January of 1942. Malcolm is the son of Mr. and Mrs. Frank Getchell of Saint Paul, Minnesota. Malcolm was a graduate of the Bemidji High School and attended Bemidji State Teachers College as well as Hamline University. Malcolm enrolled at the Bemidji State Teachers College the fall quarter of 1938 and his last quarter of attendance was the spring of 1941. Once Malcolm had enlisted, he was sent for basic training at the Maxwell Air Cadet

Field in Montgomery, Alabama. After completing his basic training Malcolm was then sent to the Midland Army Flying school at Midland, Texas for advanced training. Malcolm graduated from flying school on July 23, 1942, and received his wings as a master bombardier and aerial observer. Malcolm was then transferred to the Greenville Army Air Base, located in Greenville County, South Carolina. The Greenville Army Air Base was established in 1942 as a training base for B-25 twin-engine medium bombers. The base was renamed Greenville Air Force Base in 1947, as training bases were not in as much demand, but the base was then used as a base for transport aircraft, such as was used in the Berlin Air Lift. Malcolm flew in the same type of aircraft that Robert McPartlin flew in; McPartlin as a navigator and Getchell as a bombardier.

Historical Marker at Current Industrial Park. (Historical Marker Database. https://www.hmdb.org/m.asp?m=12118)

The local Greenville papers reported that on Wednesday, October 14, 1942, at approximately 9:30 p.m., a B-25 bomber from the Greenville Army Air Base had crashed on a routine training flight in Chester County, near the town of Richburg, South Carolina. According to the newspaper reports, all seven crewmen on board the bomber were killed in the crash. Among those listed killed was

Malcolm Getchell. There was some discrepancy in the newspaper reports as one source stated that the aircraft went down in a cleared field while another reported that the bomber stuck on a wooded hillside. The Certificate of Death states that the crash took place "in the woods."

The Greenville Piedmont, Greenville, North Carolina, October 15, 1942, p. 1.

The Getchell family was notified of Malcom's death just prior to October 16, 1942, and the *Bemidji Pioneer* ran an article on Malcom's death in the Friday, October 16, 1942, edition of the paper. In the article, it was noted that Malcom's funeral services were to be held at the Methodist church in Bemidji and services would be conducted by Dr. Crawford Grays and William Dowdell would be responsible for the military rituals of the service.

On Monday, June 7, 1943, it was announced by Dr. Charles Sattgast, university president, that, with the cooperation of the local state forestry department and forestry employee John Nelson, plans had been completed for the planting of trees on campus to honor each student or former student who was a casualty in the current war. The first dedication was to take place on Tuesday, June 8 at 2:00 p.m. on the campus. Two white pines will be planted in the memory of Malcolm Getchell and Edgar Arnold. Each tree would be marked with the student's name. The memorial tree planting was to be held in conjunction with the annual senior tree planting ceremony. The public was invited to attend the dedication ceremony. There are currently no records that show which tress may still be on campus as there is no record of the location of the tree planting locations.

As the war placed ever-increasing demands of the students at the Bemidji State Teachers College, students were very mindful of their obligation to assist in the war effort in whatever ways they could. Students created posters and decorated bulletin boards around campus to remind students of the ways they could contribute.

Bemidji State Teachers College, 1942. (Bemidji State University Library Archives)

Bemidji State Teachers College, 1942—Art Students
Posters. (Bemidji State University Archives)

Bemidji State Teachers College, 1942. (Bemidji
State University Library Archives)

The laboratory students continued to sell war bonds and
stamps during the month of October and noted that sales were as
good on Tuesday, when students were out collecting scrap, as when
classes were in session. Due to demand, sales of 50-cent, $1.00 and

$5.00 stamps would now be available. As a way of trying to increase sales, the stamp and bonds salespersons have adopted the rule that no change will be given out for use in the candy and Coca Cola vending machines unless stamps are bought first.

Photo Courtesy of the Author

October also noted the founding of the BSTC War Committee. The committee was organized by the college faculty and is designed to address curriculum, war promotional efforts and any other types of activities that may be associated with the war effort. The committee consists of Elsie Annis, A. C. Clark, A. M. Elliott, H. J. Erickson, John Glas, M. E. High, C. V. Hobson, Ruth Jessup, Margaret Kelly, Mabel Parker, and Therese Yelle.

1942 War Activities Committee. (Bemidji
State University Library Archives)

While much time and energy was devoted to addressing the
needs created by the war, the usual events that take place at the college continued much as feasible. October of 1942 noted that the six-
ty-four-member A Cappella choir performed three concerts in Bagley,
Fosston, and McIntosh under the direction of Carl O. Thompson.

At the end of November of 1942, President Sattgast announced
several new courses for the coming quarter in accordance with the
War Emergency Program. These courses were

- Military Geography,
- Mathematics Review,
- War Posters and Camouflage,
- Organization of the Armed Forces,
- Beginning Freshman English,
- Blueprint Reading, and
- Radio Code.

Students who are interested in entering the air forces were well
advised to take the following courses winter quarter as they would

be most helpful in preparing for service in that area. Those winter course offering are

- Navigation,
- Pre-flight Aeronautics, and
- Aviation Meteorology.

These courses were designed to be helpful in preparing students for active service and would be offered for the first time winter quarter to both male and female students not regularly enrolled.

November of 1942 brought on the end-of-quarter examinations, and the recognition of the eighth-grade lab students who had sold just over $1,000 worth of war bonds and stamps. The movies being shown for students until Christmas were *East of Bombay*, *Years of Progress*, and *Yours Truly*. A notice was sent out in the *Northern Student* reminding students to be patient with the arrival of journalism pins for those students who had earned them. The order was taking longer than expected due to orders from the government having priority.

December of 1942 brought several items of interest. It was reported that seventeen new students had enrolled for winter quarter classes, and President Sattgast responded to inquiries as to whether BSTC would be a military training school. President Sattgast was not optimistic about the college being accepted as such. President Sattgast noted that, due to the small size of the college and available resources, BSTC would be selected to participate in such a program. It was noted that as far as it was known, the college will continue to train fliers in its ground school in connection with actual flight training which the men receive here at the Rising School of Aviation. However, it is expected that the set up will soon cease to be a Civilian Pilot Training program and that enlistments will be taken over completely by one of the branches of the Armed Forces.

Friday night, December 11, marked the Old-Fashioned Christmas Party sponsored by the social committee. There was an informal traditional dinner that preceded the party, which was held at Sanford Hall. The party began at 8:30 p.m. and ended at midnight. The activities included games and dancing, a Grand March, a program which consisted of a Christmas message by Dr. Sattgast and a short speech on the origin of Christmas carols. There were games and dancing, being concluded by singing carols around the Christmas tree.

Faculty were asked what they wanted for Christmas, and it elicited a wide range of responses:

- "I want two weeks of sleep and money to pay my taxes."—Miss Eileen Thornton, librarian.
- "I would like to see an absolute surrender of the Axis."—Dr. A. C. Clark
- "I want a comfortable ride to Winona."—Miss Harriet Seeling, art director
- "The end of war is my greatest wish."—Miss Clara Malvey
- "I want whatever old Santa can manage, what with so many unusual orders, priorities and all."—Miss Francis McKee, junior high school supervisor[10]

Among those students listed to soon join the service was *Walter Brotherton*.

Mrs. Mary Davison of the registrar's office reported that "beginning with the current school year, all alumni and former students in the armed services will receive the *Northern Student* every month instead of four times a year as they formally have done."[11]

It was also reported that Minnesota colleges could not force students to pay an activity fee as part of registration, but if the student chose not to pay the activity fee then that student would not then be entitled to participate and receive benefits of the program.

The A Cappella choir presented their annual Christmas Concert on Sunday, December 13, at the First Lutheran Church and gave a similar concert on Wednesday, December 16, at the Bemidji High School.

---

[10] Uncredited, "What Do You Want for Christmas?" *Northern Student* (December 16, 1942), 2.

[11] Uncredited, "Alumni and Former Students Serving in the Military to Receive the *Northern Student*." *Northern Student*, Volume XVI, No. 5 (December 16, 1942), 1.

A Conservation Committee was recently organized by the student council and as was stated by student Elaine Johnson: "Now, more than ever, before, it is essential that all the citizens of this country become conservation-minded. A vital part of the nation's war effort consists of making wise use of everything, and that is exactly what conservation means. It means the wise use of time, energy, material things, and the human element to the end that the greatest possible number of present and future generations may best be served. There are many things which we, as students and faculty of this college, can do here and now to promote the cause of conservation. Our acquiring such habits of turning out lights that are not being used and being careful of school equipment would result in considerable savings. Other things we can do are collecting scrap, helping with rationing boards, using our time and energy efficiently, and taking care of our own health."[12]

The college strove to maintain an air of normalcy with maintaining as many of the extracurricular activities as possible. This included plays, concerts, and other events designed for student enjoyment.

1942 Play Scenery Production. (Bemidji State University Archives)

---

[12] Elaine Johnson, "Conservation Committee Organized," *Northern Student*, Volume XVI (December 16, 1942), 2.

President C. R. Sattgast reported that he was doubtful that the college would be given a contract for training men for the Armed Forces, citing the size of the college as an issue. President Sattgast did state that the college will continue to train future fliers in the ground school portion of the training required to receive their pilots' license; however, it was his belief that the ground training for pilots would soon be stopped and future training of pilots would be taken over by one of the branches of the military. Currently, the actual flight training was being provided by the Rising School of Aviation.

1943

WHILE JANUARY MARKED SOME REMARKABLE achievements by the students and faculty at BSTC, such as it being noted that the eighth-grade laboratory school students were over $3,000 in stamp and bond sales by January 1, 1943. It also marked one of tragedy. January would also prove to be a very deadly month for former students of the college who entered military service.

James Koefod
Died in Service January 7, 1943

It was not long into the new year of 1943 when the month of January brought more sad news of two more former students being killed in action. James Koefod was born in 1917 and registered for military service with the Army Air Corps on October 16, 1940, at the age of twenty-three. The son of local Judge and Mrs. Koefod, James was one of three brothers who had all enlisted in military service—James and David in the Air Corps and Paul in the infantry. It was noted in the local paper in October of 1942 that the three Koefod brothers had sent their father, Judge Koefod, a gold bar pin with three stars on it representing the three sons in military service. James had graduated from the Bemidji High School and Bemidji State Teachers College, at which time he attended advanced courses at the University of Minnesota. James held teaching positions until his enlistment and being sent to Chicago. Once in Chicago, James was enrolled in the Air Corps aviation program at the University of Chicago, studying meteorology. James had become ill in December, and upon admittance to a Marine hospital in Chicago, was determined to have nephritis, which is an inflammation of the kidneys.

Due to complications caused by the nephritis, James's condition worsened, and Judge and Mrs. Koefod were contact in Bemidji. James was twenty-five years old at the time of his death. Judge and Mrs. Koefod took the next available train to Chicago, but sadly arrived just several hours after James had passed away. Judge Koefod returned to Bemidji on Friday, January 8, 1943, while Mrs. Koefod and her daughter-in-law remained in Chicago to escort the body back to Minnesota for burial.

The funeral for James Koefod was held on January 10, 1943, at the Salem Lutheran Church in Rockford (which is located near Robbinsdale, Minnesota) and burial was held at the Greenwood cemetery. The Rockford paper reported the following details of the Koefod burial service:

> With full military honors, the body of James Richard Koefod, son of Judge and Mrs. S. M. Koefod of Bemidji, was laid to rest in the Greenwood cemetery near Rockford, home of his wife. Aviation Cadet Leo Meisenheimer, friend, and classmate of James, acted as military escort from Chicago and remained for the funeral which was in charge of Rev. Haar, pastor of the Salem Lutheran church of Rockford. His impressive sermon was taken from 103rd Psalm, which was James's favorite.
>
> The floral arrangements were many and beautiful and many memorials were given in his memory. Several hundred people passed by the bier. A detachment of eight servicemen from Fort Snelling acted as pallbearers, fired the salute to the dead and sounded Taps. The flag, which covered the casket, was presented to Mrs. James Koefod, the young widow, by Cadet Meisenheimer. Members of his immediate family attending the funeral were his parents, Judge and Mrs. S. M. Koefod and sister Rachel of Bemidji, Mrs. Marcel Verbrugghen (Ruth Koefod) of

Little Falls, David Koefod of Chanute Field. Paul Koefod, in officers' training at Fort Riley, Kansas, was unable to be present.[13]

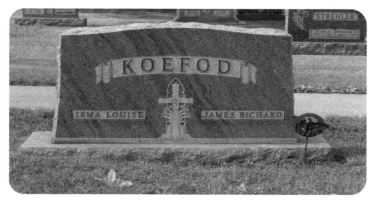

Greenwood Cemetery, Rockford, Minnesota. (Used by permission, Find A Grave member number 47592448)

Ralph Hays Goddard
Died in Service January 13, 1943

Ralph Goddard was born (there is a discrepancy on official records) either April 16 or 17, 1916, at Red Lake, Minnesota. Ralph graduated from high school in Grand Forks, North Dakota, in 1934.

Ralph aged seventeen.

---

[13] Unaccredited, "Rites for James Koefod at Rockford Sunday," *The Bemidji Daily Pioneer* (January 20, 1943).

Ralph started attending Bemidji State Teachers College in the fall semester of 1935. Ralph continued with his education through the summer session of 1939 and shortly thereafter, registered for military service.

Lt. Goddard was heavily involved in naval aircraft operations throughout his time in the pacific. Lt. Goddard was posthumously awarded the Silver Star for his actions during combat.

> Lt. (jg) Ralph H. Goddard, USNR, of Bemidji, Minnesota, posthumously, for leading his division bombers in launching an attack on a large enemy transport force, damaging two of the hostile vessels although strongly opposed by anti-aircraft fire and enemy Zero fighters, while attached to the air group of the United States aircraft carrier during an attack on Japanese naval forces off Guadalcanal on 14 and 15 November 1942. The next day, having been assigned to the task of locating and destroying an enemy shore antiaircraft installation, he deliberately placed himself in a position of great danger in order to entice the enemy to open fire and betray their position. Not succeeding in this, he searched for and found a likely target in a small clearing at the end of an obscure jungle path. Skillfully placing his bomb in the clearing, Lieutenant (jg) Goddard succeeded in destroying quantities of enemy ammunition, fuel and supplies as evidence by great fires which sprang up and spread for a distance of half a mile along the beach area.[14]

Lt. Goddard piloted a Douglas SBD-5 Dauntless Dive Bomber. The Dauntless held a crew of two, the pilot and radio operator/gun-

---

[14] Uncredited, *All Hands Naval Bulletin*, Bureau of Naval Personnel (July 1943), 61.

ner. The Dauntless proved to be a reliable and effective dive bomber and was noted for its success in the Battle of Midway.

SBD-5 Dauntless Dive Bomber. (Planes of Fame Air Museum)

Lieutenant (jg) Ralph Goddard (on right). Photo taken on January 10, 1943, on Espiritu Santo Island, South Pacific. (Uncredited Photograph—*Dauntless Helldivers*)

In the book, *Dauntless Helldivers* by Harold L. Buell, who was, at the time of Lt. Goddard's death, the Air Officer of Bombing Group

VB-10, which was based on the aircraft carrier *Enterprise*, recalled the events of Lt. Goddard's death. In summary, January 1943 found Lt. Goddard, along with the rest of the squadron, in port at the island of Espiritu Santo for resupply and repairs. While in port, the squadron commanders wanted to hold training exercises that involved night operations. That is, to take off, conduct a bombing mission and return to the carrier all during the hours of darkness. This announcement was met with little enthusiasm as there had been previously very little success with night operations from aircraft carriers.

Nonetheless, just such a training operation was slated to take place the evening of January 13, 1942. A flight test was held earlier that day by Harold Buell, and he reported that "the local weather was good, with scattered clouds and normal prevailing winds" (Harold Buell interview from *Dauntless Helldivers*). But on the return flight, Buell noted the development of a vast frontal buildup and reported this frontal buildup to his supervisors and recommended that the night training exercise scheduled for that evening be canceled.

Due to the lack of other reports of such a weather concern received by ships at sea or other aircraft, the training exercise was not canceled. So shortly after sunset, twelve aircraft lined up on the runway and took off in light rain. During the flight, a tropical storm developed over Espiritu Santo, and at time, there were sixty aircraft over the island. Due to the heavy rain, in violation of the blackout rules, several spotlights were activated on ships anchored just off shore, as well an on land, in order to help guide the aircraft safely back to the runway.

As soon as the aircraft started landing, there was a crash between two aircraft at the center of the main runway. This added more danger and delayed other aircraft from attempting a landing. After flying in extremely inclement weather for over three hours, the runway was cleared, and the remaining aircraft were cleared to land. Buell recalls, "When all aircraft had landed, it was discovered that two of the aircraft were missing. Ralph Goddard and his gunner (Charles H. O. Hamilton) had crashed in the harbor; the SBD containing their bodies was found the next morning and we buried them on a nearby hill overlooking the spot where they died so needlessly. As I recall, one or two of the fighter pilots involved in the ground crashes were killed or seriously injured."[15]

Lt. (jg) Ralph Goddard. (US Naval Archives)

On June 14, 1948, Lt. Goddard was interred at the Fort Snelling National Cemetery in Minneapolis, after being returned from Guadalcanal, Solomon Islands.

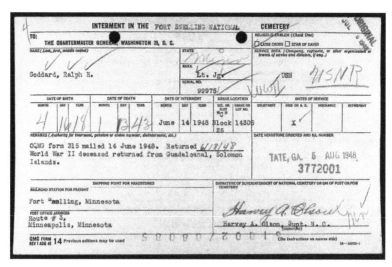

US National Cemetery Control Forms

---

[15] Harold Buell, *Dauntless Helldivers*, (New York: Crown Publishing, 1991), 171.

Edgar Arnold
Killed in Action January 17, 1943

January of 1943 was a particularly tragic month for the Bemidji State Teachers College as it had also been reported that a second former student, Edgar Arnold, had also passed away in the duty of his country.

Edgar was born on March 18, 1918, and his family moved to Bemidji from Chicago in 1936. Edgar graduated from the Bagley High School in 1937. While in high school, Edgar was an honor student and participated in chorus work and track.

Edgar Arnold was listed as one of nine students who had completed the first civil aeronautics course given at the Bemidji State Teachers College and then received their private pilots' licenses.

The nine students who have completed the first civil aeronautics course given at the Bemidji State Teachers College and who have received their private pilot's licenses are Bob Krohn, George Taylor, Ted Moleski, Gene Stish, Clifford Lunke, Edgar Arnold, Einar Sorenson, Ralph Sorvig and Harold Shellum. Mr. Rising, manager of the Bemidji Airport, was the flying instructor. (*The Bemidji Daily Pioneer*, January 22, 1943, p. 4.)

Edgar registered for the draft on October 16, 1940, entered the Naval Reserve in April of 1941 and received his initial training in Minneapolis. Edgar was then sent to the Naval Air Station in Jacksonville, Florida for additional training.

ARNOLD, EDGAR P.
Bagley, Minn.
Class 7-A

(United States Naval Archives)

He was then sent to Corpus Christi, Texas, in June of 1941 where he was commissioned as a Naval Ensign. It was at the Naval Air Station at Corpus Christi where Edgar received his aviation cadet training. Following his commission, Edgar was sent to the Coast Guard Air Station in Elizabeth City, North Carolina.

Floatplanes at Coast Guard Air Station, Elizabeth City
in March 1942. (US Navy—US Navy National Museum
of Naval Aviation photo No. 2009.006.070)

On January 17, 1943, Edgar was killed when his naval patrol aircraft crashed upon take off. The crash resulted in the death of Edgar and two other crewmen while two others were seriously injured but survived. On the death certificate, the time of the crash was listed at 05:05 a.m., and Edgar's death was a result of "Injuries, Multiple, Extreme" (North Carolina State Board of Health, Certificate of Death #374, filed January 17, 1943).

Edgar had an older brother, Sidney, who was tragically killed in an aircraft crash a few years earlier when employed as an aerial photographer for a Chicago newspaper and covering the Spanish civil war.

The Northern Student marked the death of Edgar Arnold on the front page of the Wednesday, January 27, 1943, issue. The article noted the attendance of a number of college students and teachers at the funeral service. Bob Hayes, Almond Sellem, and Blanchard Krogstad, Arnold's college mates, acted as pallbearers, and Robert Quale, college student, sang at the funeral.

It was announced that the national teacher examinations would be given at BSTC in 1943, along with Duluth and Minneapolis, in March and any graduates that wished to take the examinations would have to pay a $7.50 fee. It was noted that larger schools were increasingly requiring these examinations prior to being hired. The goal of the examinations was to raise the standards of the teaching profession and to eliminate the "dead wood" found within its ranks. The BSTC faculty were also contributing to the war effort by speaking at community events and meetings. Dr. Harold Hagg was noted to have spoken with the Solway Farm Bureau on January 29 on the topic of war bonds. The college provided programs to the public in order to support patriotism, as was shown by this article in the *Bemidji Daily Pioneer* on February 11:

> A patriotic expression of the American people through song and verse will be the theme of the assembly program to be presented at the Bemidji State teachers college Friday, Feb. 12th at 9:30 a.m. with the Alpha Phi Sigma, scholastic honor society, in charge. The public has been invited to the program.[16]

January also noted a meeting of the American Association of University Women held at the home of Mrs. J.H. Davidson; the theme of the meeting was "Women in War Time." Other topics also discussed were "Women in the Defense Industry" by Miss Mabel Croon and "Women in Other Industries" lead by Miss Myrtle Bang.

Jack McCormick
Died in Service February 16, 1943

February 1943 marked the death of another former Bemidji State Teachers College student, John (Jack) McCormick. Jack, the son of Mr. and Mrs. John McCormick of Bemidji. Mr. and Mrs. McCormick resided at 808 Irvine Avenue. Jack was known at BSTC for being an outstanding member of the Beaver basketball team, and in 1940, was named to the Moorhead All-Tournament team in 1941 after BSTC won the tournament in December of 1940, defeating

---

[16] Uncredited, *The Bemidji Daily Pioneer*, January 30, 1943.

the North Dakota Agricultural college in the finals. The accolades continued for Jack in basketball as well as football. As was noted in the March 28, 1941, edition of the *Northern Student*,

> Jack McCormick was chosen as one of three All-Conference basketball players at the guard position. Northern Teachers College All-Conference. He was also presented with the Mike Close grad trophy for having been chosen the most valuable player on the Beaver eleven by six all-conference coaches who also voted McCormick all-conference halfback last fall.

Hardware for Mac

"It was 'hardware for Mac' as Mayor Earl Bucklen presented Jack McCormick with the Mike Close Grid trophy for having been chosen the most valuable player on the Beaver eleven by six all-conference coaches who also voted McCormick all-conference halfback last fall. The presentation was made between the halves of the Bemidji-Stout cage tilt, Saturday, March 8th." *Northern Student*, Friday, March 28, 1941, p. 3. (Bemidji State University Archives)

Before coming the Bemidji State, Jack was an all-state quarterback at St. Thomas College. Jack was elected to be the "B" club President for the 1941–1942 school year. In November of 1941, Jack was playing fullback on the football team for his third year and was selected by the coaches of the Minnesota State Teachers Colleges as the honorary captain of the Teachers Colleges All-Stars. That fall, Jack was also returning to the basketball team as an All-Conference guard.

Jack enlisted in the Army Air Corps in the winter of 1941 and started training on January 16, 1942, in Sacramento, California, graduating on July 26, 1942. After his graduation in California, Jack was able to come back to Bemidji for a short visit with his parents and friends. In the January 30 edition of the *Bemidji Daily Pioneer*, it was mentioned that,

> Lieut. John F. McCormick, who graduated from the Army Air Corps school in Sacramento, Calif. last Sunday where he has been since January 16, arrived Thursday for a short visit with his mother, Mrs. John McCormick, 808 Irvine Avenue. He is being transferred to Oklahoma City and will be here until Saturday. Coming with him from the cities are his sister and husband, Mr., and Mrs. Fred Schwalin, also Mr. and Mrs. D. E. Wilfong and daughters Kathleen and Marilyn. Mrs. Wilfong is a sister of Mrs. McCormick Sr."[17]

Jack then left for his new training base in Oklahoma City.

Described in the article titled, "Thus Writes the Warrior," in the *Northern Student* in mid-February, "Lt. John McCormick in all probability had part in the recent bombings in Germany. 'Jack,' stationed in England, sent this greeting, 'From somewhere in England, the Flying Eight Ball brings best wishes for a Merry Christmas and

---

[17] Uncredited, *The Bemidji Daily Pioneer*, February 11, 1943.

Happy New Year.'"[18] Jack also wrote home and some of that news was shared with the local newspaper.

Jack wrote a letter to his mother, and parts of that letter were shared and printed in the *Bemidji Sentinel* on January 1, 1942. Jack reported that the average age of the members of his air group was twenty-one and a half years old, and his crew was known as the youngest crew in the group. Describing the aircraft he is a crew member of,

> The bomb group insignia is a flying Eight Ball which is painted on every ship. I also have one on my jacket. We can have our own personal ship name if we want to and lots of them have. Right beneath the window beside me in big letters "Black Mike" McCormick.[19]

On January 27, 1943, word had been received by Jack's relatives that he had arrived safely at his new destination (location censored). Shortly thereafter, word had been received from Jack at the college which stated under the "Thus Writes the Warrior" column,

> Flying the "Black Mike," a bomber named for him, Lt. John McCormick in all probability had part in the recent bombings in Germany. "Jack," stationed in England, sent this greeting, "From somewhere in England, the Flying Eight Ball brings best wishes for a Merry Christmas and Happy New Year." His new address may be secured from his mother.

In the February 9, 1943, edition of the *Bemidji Daily Pioneer*, it was reported,

---

[18] Uncredited, *The Northern Student*, February 17, 1943.

[19] Jack McCormick, "Jack McCormick Tells of Life in England," *Bemidji Sentinel*, January 1, 1942, 1.

> A letter just received from Lieut. Jack McCormick
> tells of a recent trip to London where six officers
> enjoyed a two-day leave. His interesting letter
> graphically describes the shows they were able
> to see and their enjoyment of a large hotel and
> its luxuries that they had not been enjoying in
> camp.[20]

The tragic news regarding Jack was posted in the February 24, 1943, edition of the *Northern Student*.

> Word has been received here by Mrs. John
> McCormick from the war department that her
> son, Lieut. Jack McCormick has been reported
> missing in action in the western European area
> since Feb. 16. Lieut. McCormick, who was sta-
> tioned in England with the air corps, is a gradu-
> ate of the Bemidji High School and had attended
> the Bemidji State Teachers College before he
> enlisted. Here he was a member of the Bemidji
> Beaver football squad and the basketball team
> and is shown below in his basketball uniform.
> He had also attended St. Thomas college and
> the University of Minnesota before coming to
> the Bemidji college. Lieut. McCormick had been
> with the air corps for over a year and had been
> overseas for the past several months.[21]

At the end of March 1943, Lt. McCormick was awarded, post-humously, the Air Medal by headquarters of the Eighth Air Force. Lt. McCormick's address at that time was listed as 818 Irvine Avenue, Bemidji, Minnesota.

---

[20] Uncredited, *Bemidji Daily Pioneer*, January 30, 1943, 2.
[21] Uncredited, "Thus Writes the Warrior," *The Bemidji Daily Pioneer*, February 9, 1943.

The final mention of Lt. Jack McCormick was in the *Bemidji Daily Pioneer* in the Friday evening, March 17, 1944:

> Memorial services for Lieut. Jack McCormick were conducted Friday morning at Requiem High Mass at the St. Phillips church with the Rev. Fraling in charge of the service. The mass was sung by the students of the St. Phillips school. Out-of-town relatives here for the services were Mrs. D. Wilfong, St. Paul, and Mrs. Anna Mosher, Stillwater, aunts of Lieut. McCormick. Lieut. McCormick who had attended school and college in Bemidji, has been officially reported missing in action, according to word received here by his mother, Mrs. John McCormick. He has been missing since Feb. 16, 1943, during an operational flight over Europe. He had been awarded the air medal and Purple Heart. His brother Hugh and sister Mrs. Fred Schwalen make their home in Bemidji.

Meanwhile life at BSTC continued with lamentations by the student body that while many would not consider significant, were noteworthy to the student body. One such example is provided:

"Just Comment"
Mona Hoganson

> The increasing lack of male students was evident in not only statistical terms but by the lamentations of the female student body. The fellows are leaving our midst at a rapid pace…looks as if we girls will be doing the "howling" from here on in. Heaven help the male who ventures to put his foot inside the door of this institution come spring…a reception committee in the form of a

pack of lonely fems comparable to the most for-
midable "wolves" will be waiting with pointed
ears.[22]

February marked a critical teacher shortage nationally, where it
was estimated that, due to men and women entering military service
or war support employment, there would be a shortage of between
50,000 to 100,00 teachers. Mr. F. R. Adams, State Director of the
Division of Teacher Personnel, says: "In my opinion, the teacher
shortage in Minnesota will be more acute next fall than most people
realize."[23] Former teachers were asked to take a refresher course and
renew their certificates, and high school seniors were encouraged to
become teachers.

The major winter quarter party was sponsored by the WAA
(Women's Athletic Association) and the "B" club on February 13.
The party consisted of a mixture of sports, a dinner, and a social
dancing party. Skiing, ice skating, tobogganing, and cardboard slid-
ing was enjoyed in the afternoon followed by a dinner held at the
cafeteria consisting of baked beans, wieners, hot buns, celery, carrots,
milk, and coffee. For dessert, there was ice cream and cake, followed
by social dancing in the gym to jukebox records while other games
such as shuffleboard and ping-pong were played in the cafeteria.

Another example of the continuing efforts made by student
organizations was a rummage sale that was held on February 27 by
the Alpha Phi Sigma college honor society, in which all proceeds
would be used to benefit the college men serving in the armed forces.
In 1942, the proceeds from the annual rummage sale was used for
purchasing war bonds and years prior to the war the proceeds were
used to purchase books for the college library as well as a silver plaque
that lists the outstanding senior of each year.

The college was now faced with the sad task of remembering and
honoring those former students who had been killed in action. The first
such notice in the student paper came at the end of February 1943.

---

[22] Mona Hoganson, "Just Comment," *The Northern Student*, February 24, 1943.
[23] F. R. Adams, "Teacher Shortage," *The Northern Student*, February 24, 1943, 2.

The deaths of two former BSTC students, Lieut. Ralph Goddard and James Koefod, have been announced. Word has been received for the U.S. Navy, division of Aeronautics, that Lieut. Ralph Goddard, son of A. C. Goddard, 2319 Birchmont Drive, was killed in action January 13 and that his death came as a result of an airplane crash. He was with VB-Squadron 10. When heard from last, he was thought to be stationed in Guadalcanal. He was a graduate of the Grand Forks high school and attended the Bemidji State Teachers College. He had his training at Wold-Chamberlin field in Minneapolis and at Pensacola, Florida.

James Koefod passed away January 7 at the Marine hospital, Chicago, from nephritis complications. He had been in the hospital for the past month for observation. He was an aviation cadet in training at the University of Chicago. James was a graduate of the Bemidji high school and a degree graduate of the Bemidji State Teachers College. He took advanced work at the University of Minnesota and had held teaching positions since his graduation before entering training in Chicago.[24]

More sad news was received by the family of Jack McCormick when Jack was reported missing in action. Word had been received by Jack's mother, Mrs. John McCormick from the war department that Jack had been missing in action over western Europe since February 16. No further word had been received by the McCormick family, and on March 17, 1942, memorial services were held for Jack at the St. Phillips church in Bemidji. At the service that Friday morning at Requiem High Mass, conducted by Rev. Fraling, the mass was sung by the students of the St. Phillips School. Jack had been awarded the

---

[24] Uncredited, "In Memorandum," *The Northern Student*, February 24, 1943, 3.

Air Medal and the Purple Heart posthumously in a ceremony held by the Eighth Air Force on March 30, 1943. The Air Medal is awarded to those who have exhibited exceptionally meritorious achievement; for bomber aircrew, it constituted five combat missions over enemy territory or for the destruction of an enemy aircraft.

John F. (Jack) McCormick. *The Northern Student*, February 24, 1943. (Bemidji State University Archives)

As the war continued, the students of the Bemidji State Teachers College continued to contribute however they could to the war effort. The War Activities Committee of the Student Council was now working with the Red Cross by students giving speeches at various city gatherings to spread information about the work of the red cross as well as arranging for students to assist with making surgical dressings.

Of extremely important news to the college was the news that the college had received full accreditation by the North Central

Association. There were three new benefits that were outlined by President C. R. Sattgast as a result of such accreditation:

1. Credits received at BSTC will be accepted without probation in all other colleges in the North Central Association.
2. Graduates from BSTC will be acceptable as teachers in all North Central Association member schools.
3. The North Central Association furnishes a standard by which the college may measure its worth and make plans for further progress and improvement.

North Central Association

—Courtesy of Duluth Herald News Service

Heading from the North Central Association report, President C. R. Sattgast is shown announcing to the Student Council that the college has received full accreditation by the association. Left to right from the presi- | dent are Butler Spaulding of Osakis, junior class representative; Dorothy Satterholm of Baudette, council president; Dr. C. V. Hobson, personnel director; Priscilla Hepokoski of Menahga, social committee chairman; | Florian Karnowski of Little Falls, freshman class representative; Mildred Kerhuem of Osakis, secretary; and Renville Lund of Bemidji, vice-president. Also on the student council, but not pictured, is Elaine Dearholt, chairman of the war service committee.

The Northern Student, Volume XVI Tuesday, April 13, 1943, p. 1. (Bemidji State University Archives)

A student, Mona Hoganson, wrote in the April 13, 1943, edition of the *Northern Student* some of the concerns that were held by students at the time, in addition to those caused by the war.

> Occasionally, something which can become a controversial subject arise here in school. Such a situation now exists. The problem of student's leaving school and going home frequently during

weekends has caused concern among the faculty and among others. There are two main objections to this situation. First, the student loses contact with his fellow students and instructors. Invariably the important social events of the school year occur during the weekends. The second point, and that which seemingly most important, is the fact that the student will not develop self-reliance if he cannot stay at school without travelling home often. Self-confidence and self-reliance are two of the most important elements which one can attain from college. It's something to think about.[25]

The track team won the 1943 Northern Division Teachers conference track meet held at the BSTC track, and because the Bemidji team's total points exceeded the total made by the winner of the southern division, the BSTC team was named state champion. Many organizations held elections for officers for the upcoming school year, the Women's Athletic Association and Association for Childhood Education being a few. The "B" club sponsored the last school dance that was held in the college gym on Friday, May 28. The music was provided by a twelve-piece orchestra from the high school. While the last event held by the "B" club was a picnic on June 4 where new faculty members were guests.

As was tradition, each year, President Sattgast held a dinner for all of the faculty and their spouses. This was a formal affair, and the expectation was that all faculty would attend. This usually included the introduction of the new faculty and a speech by the president on the academic year.

---

[25] Mona Hoganson, "Just Comment," *The Northern Student*, April 13, 1943, 2.

1942 President Sattgast's Faculty Dinner.
(Bemidji State University Archives)

While April of 1943 was thankfully lacking in news of the deaths of any BSTC students or faculty, the month of May was not as kind.

Kenneth Olson
Missing in Action/Died in Service May 19, 1943

Kenneth Olson, son of Emma Olson of Nymore, attended the Bemidji High School where he was heavily involved in athletics as well as a member of the National Honor Society. After graduation from high school Kenneth enrolled at the Bemidji State Teachers College, where he was a member of the Beaver football team.

Kenneth registered for the draft on October 16, 1940, in Grygla, Minnesota, listing himself as being 5'11" tall and weighing 160 pounds.

(National Archives and Records Administration. www.archives.gov)

After Kenneth entered the military he was accepted by the Army Air Corps for training as a pilot.

> Kenneth A. Olson, son of Mrs. Emma Olson, Nymore, is a member of a class of student officers and aviation cadets to be graduated soon from the Air Force Advanced Flying School at Stockton Field, CA. The graduates will be commissioned as Second Lieutenants in the Air Force Reserve and will be given the silver wings, symbolic of the aeronautical rating of a pilot. They will be placed on active duty with their new rank in the Army Air Force. Before entering the final and advanced course Aviation Cadet Olson completed 20 weeks of primary training at the Viaslia-Dinuba School of Aeronautics, Viaslia, Cal., and Minter Field, Bakersfield, Cal. Cadet Olson was graduated from the Bemidji High School in 1938 and attended Bemidji State Teachers College.[26]

---

[26] Uncredited, "Our Men in Service," *The Bemidji Daily Pioneer*, July 21, 1942, 2.

Kenneth had written to his mother and told her that he expected to be transferred to Salt Lake City for additional training and then planned to make a visit home after that.

Kenneth completed his pilot's training for piloting the B-24 Liberator, which is a heavy bomber. Kenneth was assigned to the Ninetieth Heavy Bomb Group, the "Jolly Rogers."

B-24 Liberator of the Ninetieth Bomb Group—"Jolly Rogers" (World War Photos, https://www.worldwarphotos.info/gallery/usa/ aircrafts-2-3/b-24-liberator/b-24-liberator-193-90-bomb-group/)

The Jolly Rogers were stationed in the southwest Pacific from 1942 through 1944. Often deployed from Australia to smaller bases on pacific islands as they were liberated by allied forces. Kenneth and his bomb group were stationed at the 5 Mile Drome near Port Moresby, Papua New Guinea. The base was called the five mile as that was approximately how far the base was from Port Moresby, but it was also known as Wards Airfield in honor of Australian Lieutenant Colonel Kenneth Harry Ward, who was heavily involved in the construction of the 5 Mile Drome and was later killed on August 27, 1942, in fighting at Isurava during a series of battles along the Kododa Trail in the Australian Territory of Papua.

5 Mile Drome—"Wards Airfield." (United States Army Air Forces—United States Army Air Forces photograph)

The Jolly Rogers were stationed at Wards Airfield from 1942 through most of 1944. Below is the crew of B-24 #41-24269. Kenneth Olson is the Co-Pilot located on the center of the top row.

B-24 #41-24269 Captained by Lt. Donald D. Almond. (Photograph from slide received by United States Army Air Force Public News Board from the Fifth Air Force dated June 4, 1943. United States Army Air Forces photograph)

According to Army Air Force records the crew was responsible for the following actions prior to the aircraft being brought down.

- Destroyed twenty-one enemy aircraft
- Probably destroyed twelve enemy aircraft
- Sank seven enemy vessels
- Damaged on enemy vessel.

In the May 29, 1943, Saturday evening edition of the *Bemidji Daily Pioneer*, the article headline read,

> TWO LOCAL MEN MISSING IN ACTION. Telegrams have been received by parents of two Bemidji men, Kenneth Olson and Stanley Carter, stating that both are missing in action with the United States Army Air Corps. Lieut. Olson, son of Mrs. Emma Olson of Nymore, has been missing since May 19th, somewhere in the southwest pacific. He is a graduate of the Bemidji high school, where he was prominent in athletic activities and was a member of the National Honor Society. Following his graduation in 1938, he attended the Bemidji State Teachers College until he joined the service. He was a member of the Beaver football team while at college.[27]

On May 7, the Almond crew slated for a bombing mission to Madang (located on the north coast of Papua New Guinea), but the aircraft got stuck in the mud at the runway and was unable to participate. On May 19, 1943, B-24D-24269, led by Lt. Almond and crewed by Lt. Kenneth Olson, took off from 5 Mile Drome at 05:15 a.m. on a daylight reconnaissance mission along the northeast coast of New Guinea. Approximately an hour and thirty-five minutes into the mission, the aircraft was attacked by five Japanese Mitsubishi A6M5 "Zekes." The transmission received by the airfield at 09:10 a.m. from Olson's aircraft was "ATTACKED BY 5 ZEKES." The aircraft

---

[27] Unaccredited, "Two Local Men Missing in Action," *The Bemidji Daily Pioneer*, May 29, 1943.

crewed by Kenneth was eventually rammed by one of the Japanese aircraft, which was piloted by Sergeant Hikoto Sato of the Twenty-Fourth Sentai (squadron). The last transmission received from Olson's aircraft was at 09:21 a.m. stating, "S O S GOING DOWN." Here is the report of what took place after the last transmission from the Kenneth Olson aircraft.

> Upon receipt of Almond's last message, a P-38 ("Lightning" fighter aircraft) was dispatched immediately to search the area but found nothing. By 1130 the 400th squadron sent Lieutenants Porter, Martin, and Menge, with Capt. Thornhill flying with Menge, to cover a wider area, but they found nothing. The next day, in inclement weather Thornhill and Porter were back in the vicinity of Madang looking for Almond when they were jumped by nine Zeros. They had to fight their way home and the Japs lost three Zeros to their guns. Both aircraft were damaged by the fighters. Notwithstanding the diligent searches, nothing was ever found of Almond's aircraft.[28]

Mitsubishi A6M5 'Zeke." (Planes of Fame Air Museum. https://planesoffame.org/aircraft/plane-A6M5)

---

[28] Wiley Woods, *Legacy of the 90th Bombardment Group "The Jolly Rogers,"* (Paducah, Kentucky: Turner Publishing Company, 1994), 57.

SCMP

It is estimated that the bomber went down in the pacific somewhere in the vicinity of Karkar Island. (*South China Morning Post*, April 23, 2013)

The Japanese aircraft piloted by Sgt. Sato also went down after ramming Olson's aircraft and was never located while a captured Japanese document dated May 1943, reported that "the plane of Sgt. Maj. Kira, which was attached to that Air Brigade (SHIROGANE Air Brigade) attacked three B-24's in the vicinity of Madang, shot down two (of these one is uncertain), and inflicted damage on the other one."[29] Possibly this document also refers to Almond's aircraft, but without the exact date of Kira's encounter it cannot be determined. The crew of the bomber that was lost that day were,

> Pilot: 1st Lieutenant Donald O. Almond. From South Dakota
> Co-Pilot: 2nd Lieutenant John J. Cahill. From Oregon
> Crew: 2nd Lieutenant Robert L. McClure. From Ohio
> Crew: 2nd Lieutenant Kenneth A. Olson. From Minnesota
> Crew: T/Sgt Forrest D. Wright. From Illinois
> Crew: T/Sgt Ivan O. Sand. From Minnesota
> Crew: S/Sgt Marvin C. Parsons. From District of Columbia

---

[29] *Ibid.*, 58.

Crew: S/Sgt. Oliver R. Neese. From Indiana
Crew: S/Sgt. Maurice Derfler. From Pennsylvania
Crew: Cpl. Joseph L. Wagner. From Texas.[30]

Kenneth and the drew of the bomber were not officially declared by the military until December 19, 1945. Kenneth was awarded the Purple Heart.

Kenneth and his crew are memorialized at the Manila American Cemetery and Memorial on the Walls of the Missing.

(Manila American Cemetery and Memorial—Walls of the Missing)

Kenneth's family also had a marker placed at the Greenwood Cemetery in Bemidji following the news of Kenneth's death.

Greenwood Cemetery, Bemidji, Minnesota

---

30 Russell S. Pickett, "WWII Memorial Pages," RussPickett. http://russpickett.com/.

This plaque was placed at the Wright Patterson Air Force Base by the Ninetieth Bomb Group Association in 1985.

Kenneth Olson is listed as the 232nd casualty of the Ninetieth Bomb Group, the Jolly Rogers, of World War II.

"Daggy Writes from South Pacific Area"

Ensign R. H. Daggy, who is an ensign in the Navy currently serving in the South Pacific, writes that he was visited by several BSTC students and faculty. Ensign Daggy writes that he was visited by Will Erickson, the former Northern Student editor, who stopped at the lab to see Daggy, but unfortunately he was not around at the time.[31]

The week of June 6, 1943, marked the graduation of sixty-two students. Sixteen of those graduates were awarded baccalaureate degrees. The baccalaureate address was delivered by the Rev. Abner Haugen of Crookston at the First Lutheran Church. The four-year graduates honored the traditional skip day on May 27. The "B" club threw a clam bake on the twenty-eighth, and it was noted that the

---

[31] R. H. Daggy, "Daggy Writes from South Pacific Area," Unaccredited. *The Northern Student,* June 8, 1943, 2.

band was good and that Dr. Sauer and his wife "were tearing up huge chunks of the carpet."[32] It was noted that in Sanford Hall, the dormitory for female students, that spring brought mumps, poison ivy, arthritis, and stiff necks. The song, "Back in the Saddle Again" was popular, and students were lamenting the fact that they had to clean their rooms before checkout and how did they ever collect so much stuff over the year?

On June 8, through the cooperation of the State Forestry department, plans have been completed for the planning of tress on the college campus for each casualty of a student or former student in the current war. President Sattgast announced that the first dedication will take place with the planting of two white pine trees in remembrance of Edgar Arnold and Malcolm Getchell. Each tree will be marked with the student's name. The public was invited to attend the dedication service.

In the section of the student paper entitled, "Thus Writes the Warrior," Lt. Harry Roese, Jr. writes, "I appreciate your thoughtfulness in remembering the Bemidji alumni who have gone overseas. There are quite a few men here from Minnesota, and we all have enjoyed reading the splendid paper. Thank you for remembering us, and we will not forget that we are fighting for you and the posterity you are building."[33]

There was a supplement added to the June 8, 1943, edition of the *Northern Student* entitled "Honor Roll of Our Service Men," which listed the names and contact information (when allowed, those serving overseas could not list their address). Those listed as being deceased or missing in action at that time were,

- Edgar Arnold (Deceased)
- Malcom Getchell (Deceased)
- Lt. John F. McCormick (Missing)

---

[32] United States Army Air Corps. Missing Air Crew Report (MACR). Filed August 25, 1943.

[33] Harry Roese, "Thus Writes the Warrior," *The Northern Student,* June 8, 1943, 2.

Harry Roese
Died in Service August 25, 1943

While a student at the Bemidji State Teachers College, Harry was noted for being a member of the college's rifle team. Harry enlisted in the Army Air Corps on November 8, 1940.

Shortly after becoming a member of the Army Air Forces in 1942, Harry was sent to Helena, Arkansas, for training as an aerial gunner in an observation squadron. Harry reported to his parents that he expected to be sent in August to another flying base to receive his ten days of acrobatic flying, which would then entitle him to be pursue his pilot's wings. Harry was then sent to a ten-week advanced flying school program at Blytheville, Arkansas.

Harry's participation with the college rifle team paid dividends when it was reported in October of 1942 that he has set a new Army Air Force record for marksmanship with a score of 298 of a possible 300 in when he was in a competition at the Blytheville, Arkansas, flying school. After Harry completed his training at Blytheville, he was transferred to Kaye Field, Columbus, Mississippi, for final training. In November of 1942, Mr. and Mrs. Roese moved to Crookston, Minnesota, and there learned in December that Harry had earned his pilot's wings in a ceremony at Kay Field, located in Columbus, Mississippi.

In January of 1943, Mr. and Mrs. Roese reported to the *Bemidji Daily Pioneer* that Lt. Roese was now located at Homestead, Florida, with the Air Transport Command, where he is taking an intense course in instrument flying.

TRAINING IN FLORIDA

LT. HARRY E. ROESE, Jr., son of Mr. and Mrs. Harry E. Roese, Sr., former residents of Bemidji, is now located at Homestead, Fla., with the Air Transport command, where he is taking an intensive course in instrument flying. The Roese family now resides at Crookston, where Mr. Roese is athletic coach for the Northwest School of Agriculture.

The Bemidji Daily Pioneer, January 11, 1943.

In April of 1943, Mr. and Mrs. Roese had heard from their son that he was now stationed "somewhere" in India. In June, Lieutenant Roese was informed by his parents that his nephew, Bud, who was also a pilot, had been killed in action and that Harry's father and sister, Betty, planned to go to Hazel, Minnesota, where services were to be held.

Lieutenant Roese was assigned to the Fifty-Seventh Ferry Squadron, flying cargo and personnel from India to China, flying over the extremely dangerous route through the Himalayan mountains, known to airmen as "The Hump." On August 25, 1943, Lieutenant Roese left the airbase located Mohanbari, Assam (Calcutta, India), at 07:20 a.m., piloting a C-47 (serial number 41-18543) carrying cargo for China. The other crew members were Flight Officer Marion L. Meaders, from Newton, Mississippi, and Private First Class Charles W. Locke, from Atoka, Oklahoma. The Military Missing Air Crew Report does not show where or how the aircraft was last seen after leaving Calcutta. According to the information received by the Roese family, the flight of several aircraft on the same mission turned back to base due to encountering stormy weather. It was believed that

Roese's aircraft was blown off course by the inclement weather, and the investigation as to the crash stated that natives had heard the sputtering of aircraft engines high over the mountains and heard a boom which "shook the entire valley."[34] Upon arriving at the crash scene, it was found that Lieutenant Roese had been thrown clear of the aircraft upon crashing and had shown burned legs. In a letter sent to the Roese family by one of Lieutenant Roese's friends, Lieutenant P. S. Shafer, Shafer wrote that he visited the town close to where the accident took place and two missionaries there told Lieutenant Shafer that Lieutenant Roese and the two other crewmen had been given military funerals and buried there. The three crewmen were listed as killed in action (KIA). Lieutenant Harry E. Roese Jr. received the Distinguished Flying Cross and Air Medal and had been recommended for the China Flying Cloud decoration. The Roese family suffered doubly as their two sons, Harry and Bud, who were both military pilots, were killed in action serving their country. Lieutenant Roese is buried at the Fort Snelling National Cemetery, located in Minneapolis, Minnesota.

C-47 "Goonie Bird." (United States Air Force photograph)

---

[34] United States Army Air Corps, Missing Air Crew Report (MACR), filed August 25, 1943.

HARRY ROESE, JR. was the first son of a Bemidji Legionnaire to make the supreme sacrifice during World War II, according to Adjutant Joe Hartness, who said that on Aug. 25, 1943, Lieutenant Roese was transporting supplies from India to China when his plane crashed in a mountain storm. His dad has been a Legionnaire for more than 25 years.

Legionnaire, Minnesota Legion, September 1943.

On August 23, 1943, the State Teachers College Board granted military leave of absence to BSTC President C. E. Sattgast. Dr. Sattgast had been sworn into the Army as a captain and will be working with the Reserve American Military Government of Occupied Territories and his commission in the Army will extend for the duration of the war, plus an additional six months, or at the discretion of the president. Captain Sattgast will initially be sent for training at the University of Virginia and the probably to Oxford, England, prior to being assigned a duty station. Dr. A. C. Clark was elected the new president of the Bemidji State Teachers College in the absence of Dr. Sattgast. In a statement of policy, President Clark declared, "The Bemidji State Teachers College, in common with all other institutions, is doing and will continue to everything in its power to help with the war effort."[35] Dr. Clark also acknowledged the dire need for

[35] A. C. Clark, "Dr. Sattgast Given Leave of Absence, Dr. Clark Appointed College President." *The Bemidji Daily Pioneer*, August 24, 1943, 1.

teachers in the country as well as the state. In Minnesota alone, there was a reported shortage of between 2500–3000 teachers.

Dr. A. C. Clark. (Bemidji State University Archives)

The start of the 1943–1944 academic year marked a new high number of scholarships (seven) that were being made available to students. However, as reported by the college registrar, Miss Mabel Parker, enrollment had dropped from last fall with only around 127 students registered this fall, and of that number only eighteen to twenty were male students. The founding and first appearance of the male chorus was announced with their first performance to be held at the school assembly on October 1. There was discussion in the student paper promoting inter-collegiate sports for women as well as "dorm chatter" involving everything from the rising bell that sounds at 06:30 a.m. to pranks around the dorm that included everything from short-sheeted beds to alarm clocks being set to go off in the middle of the night.

Dr. Sattgast, who has been the past president of the Bemidji State Teachers College for the past five years, left the campus September 20, 1943, for military service. President Sattgast will be in the Army as a rank of captain and will be training to work with the AMGOT (Allied Military Government for Occupied Territories). It was noted that Dr. Sattgast will resume the presidency of the college when his military service is no longer required.

The 1943 BSTC football team was comprised of fourteen players, which includes four returning players. For the first time, the BSTC football team will be the only teachers' college that will play only other colleges. The first college picnic was held in chilly weather on September 9, where several faculty members and their wives served the students after a few games designed to get the blood flowing. It was noted that while everyone at first attempted to eat corn-on-the-cob in a dignified manner, eventually everyone gave up and resorted the two-handed method of "biting and gnawing." While the war created a drop in male students, athletics on campuses continued to be emphasized as essential. "By continuing football and intercollegiate sports, BSTC is directly in line with the nation's physical fitness program as outlined by War Manpower Czar Paul V. McNutt. McNutt recommended that colleges, high schools, and all athletic organizations should continue their sports program 'as a mark of patriotism.'"[36]

The traditional Homecoming events held every fall were replaced by "Beaver Day" activities that were slated to take place on Thursday and Friday, October 7 and 8. The festivities started with a pow-wow at the college fireplace which include a bonfire, college yells, the selection of an all-school queen and community sing. The football players for that fall were also announced. Each club submitted a candidate for queen, who was selected by a secret committee made up of two faculty members and two students. The two-day event included a "Victory" talk by football Coach Erickson and a Harvest dance.

At Halloween, there was a Halloween Feast and party held in the dormitory dining room and those who attended were greeted by a white-sheeted student at the door to the dining room, which was decorated with black cats, witches, and lighted jack-o-lanterns. After the dinner, the students enjoyed games, dancing, and bobbing for apples. Dessert was provided after each person had been successful

---

[36] Paul V. McNutt, *The Northern Student*, September 29, 1943, 4.

in bobbing for an apple. The dorm girls sang and told ghost stories around the fireplace

Students were informed that the drama department now had a recording machine so students could make recordings of their voice. This would be especially valuable to future teachers in foreign languages and speech fundamentals. The cost for a recording on both sides of the seven-inch record at 78 rpm was twenty cents and was taken from a student's deposit fee.

In the fall of 1943, the laboratory school was operating at full steam as the shortage of teachers was very evident and teachers were in great demand, especially in the rural areas of the state. The grade school students who were part of the laboratory school to serve as students for the BSTC students were taught many skills that were not strictly related to more traditional knowledge-based skills, as seen in the photograph below.

Bemidji State Teachers College Laboratory School
1943. (Bemidji State University Archives)

Bemidji State Teachers College Laboratory School
1943. (Bemidji State University Archives)

The war was a shadow that acted a constant reminder of the sacrifices being made by the BSTC former students, faculty, and staff. This article, as printed in the *Northern Student* epitomizes this awareness.

"Time is your most valuable possession, my boy." Thus spoke the dignified old gentleman as he handed a round gold watch to the carefree smiling youth, who didn't fully realize the importance of such a valuable gift from such a revered uncle. But he kept the watch with him for years, and when he enlisted in the army air corps, the heirloom was a part of his small collection of personal possessions. There were weeks when the safety of the timepiece was threatened…especially in the jungles of New Guinea. Heat and humidity do strange things to gold. In his new surroundings the young pilot finally came to the realization of the wonderful and terrible meanings of time… precious time in which to work; horrible time in which to kill. Once in a while he wondered how much time the people back home had to help. One of his sister's letters mentioned her surgical dressing work. He smiled grimly but was glad. Yes, surgical dressings helped for they were needed. Months passed. One night after a routine enemy raid, the exhausted pilot returned to his tent only to find that it had been destroyed by a Jap bomb. In the heat of the oppressive dawn, he searched among the debris for a small object. He had to recover it. No, he didn't find a gold watch, but he DID find a charred lump of blackened steel and gold. He clutched it in his hand and looked up at the gray sky…wondering. To the reader: This is a true account of a former student now a pilot in the army air corps. Let's help him and others like him by making surgical dressings…as many as we can. These men are giving ALL their time to their country. How much are you giving?[37]

Another faculty member, Dr. Harold T. Hagg, left for military service on October 18, 1943, for training in the United States Navy. Prior to leaving for military duty Dr. Hagg was the chairman of the social studies division and had been at BSTC since 1936.

Dr. Harold T Hagg. (Bemidji State University Archives)

---

[37] Uncredited, "For Him and Others Like Him," *The Northern Student*, October 27, 1943, 3.

Due to the shortage of labor available during the war years, everyone was required to do more than normally would be expected. It was noted that Mrs. Soland, one of the college secretaries had missed a day of work in late October, not to play some sort of "hooky," but to help on her father's farm outside of Bemidji, harvesting potatoes. Due to a lack of manpower, Mrs. Soland did her patriotic bit by spending the day picking potatoes, and when asked how many she thought she had picked she replied, "I don't know, but the way I felt, it must have been nearly five or six hundred." She also remarked, "It's hard work, but then, it's lots of fun."[38] It was noted that Mrs. Soland was one of the service wives at the college, her husband being in the Army.

Ensign *Bob Frazer* was on campus in October and had just returned from the Southwest Pacific after being in battle in the Guadalcanal and Solomon Islands vicinity as a naval aviator. Bob returned home with the remaining member of his squadron, and after a short time in Bemidji, was now in San Diego awaiting orders for possible further combat duty.

By the end of November, the year's social events had been planned out. The annual Christmas party, a second winter quarter party was planned for February and was arranged by the freshman class. The spring party to be held in March was under the direction of the sophomore class and Guest Day would be sponsored by the junior and senior classes. The fall picnic, Beaver Day party, and the tea given for the alumni made up the all-college parties and would be sponsored by the social committee.

November also marked a jewelry-for-servicemen collection at the dormitory, under the supervision of Eva Mae Cann. It was reported that a sizable collection of pins, bracelets, necklaces, etc. were collected by the girls, though most of them claimed that the "real junk" was at home. Any student who had made a donation was asked to wear that item to dinner the night before the national drive closed.

November was also marked by the eighth-grade laboratory class having sold $3,284.10 in stamps and bonds since the sale started in early October. The stamps and bonds are sold in the college lobby on

---

[38] Uncredited, *The Northern Student*, November 24, 1943, 2.

Tuesdays from 12:30 p.m. to 1:10 p.m. Also in support of the war effort were the 3,590 four-by-four surgical bandages made during the six meetings this academic year at the college Red Cross room by student volunteers. It was reported that 132 volunteers put in 244 hours creating the bandages. The Red Cross room was open Mondays and Fridays work volunteers to make the bandages.

It was made note of in the student paper that "*Kenny Gregg*, who recently visited BSTC, must have found the hunting pretty good while out west because he now receives mail addressed to Mr. and Mrs. Gregg… It really is 'amusin' but confusin'" how the freshman girls find out the names of the fellows who are back on furloughs."[39] Kenneth Gregg visited the campus the week prior from Sheppard Field, California, after being commissioned a second lieutenant in the Army Air Corps. *The Northern Student* reported, "War department bulletins have been received concerning cadets Kenneth Gregg and Douglas Wachs. In the near future, Cadet Gregg, member of a class of student officers and aviation cadets in the Army Air Forces Advanced Flying School at Stockton Field, California, will be made a full-fledged pilot and receive his coveted silver wings. Before entering the course at Stockton Field, Kenny Gregg completed eighteen weeks of primary and basic training at Twenty-Nine Palms and Lemoore, California. After graduation he will be placed on active duty in his rank with the Army Air Forces."[40]

As Thanksgiving 1943 approached, the war gave everyone time to reflect and realize what they had to be thankful for. Here are just a few of the reasons to be thankful that were quoted in the student paper the week of Thanksgiving:

> With an empty place at the table and much more
> in our hearts, we can yet approach Thanksgiving
> in 1943 with much to be thankful for. Liberty,
> home, friends, love, pity, tolerance, the grandeur
> of trees, the beauty of snow, the fragrance of

---

[39] Uncredited, *The Northern Student*, November 24, 1943, 2.
[40] Uncredited, *The Northern Student*, November 24, 1943, 4.

flowers, rainbows, the good smell of old clothes, sleep, the downiness of blankets, the smell of dew-sprinkled grass, the purity of washed clothes hung out to dry, the toothless smile of a baby, the fragrance of fresh bread, the comfort of the night, children's laughter, the strength in "The Lord is my Shepard," the symmetry of new-plowed fields, the whinny of a horse, the privilege of being an American, the aroma of "moms" cooking, the thrill of a book, the serenity of the sky, flirting stars, life and eternity beyond-for these we thank Thee, O Lord. Coupled with our thanks is a pledge that there will be fewer empty places at America's Thanksgiving tables next year.

Miss Margaret Kelly summarized her idea of an offering of thanks by saying that Americans might pause to be thankful for the safety that the government has provided them; for the opportunity of helping the war effort by doing something useful here; for the privilege of seeing friends as they return on furloughs; for the rationing and price control programs which have protected American food supply.

Donna Mikkola, whose husband is already overseas, find consolation in the knowledge that the end of the war is coming, or at least that it is no longer the beginning. It is Joyce Worth's sincere feeling that the very sacrifices that Americans are called upon to make are something for them to be thankful for, because in making them, they know that they are helping to heed the cries of the needy and conquered peoples, and that they

are helping to restore justice to what promises to
be a better world.[41]

On occasion some of the students or faculty who had enlisted
were able to visit the college while on furlough. One such case was a
visit to the college by Lieutenant Richard Daggy on December 14. Lt.
Daggy, who had left his teaching position in the science department,
spoke that evening at the college theater. Lt. Daggy told of his experiences while serving in the South Pacific. "One of my most exciting
experiences while serving in the South Pacific came when I was lost
alone on a jungle island."[42] Lt. Daggy was tasked with the control of
mosquitoes while being assigned to United States Navy. Lt. Daggy
was stationed in the New Hebrides, south of Guadalcanal, but visited
many of the smaller surrounding islands to continue his work.

Other BSTC faculty had also volunteered for duty in the military. Robert B. Frost, who was the chairman of the physical education division, is a captain in the Army and served at the Army Air
Forces Tactical Center at Orlando, Florida since 1942 and served
as a physical training officer, theater officer, army emergency relief
officer, and insurance officer.

Captain E. W. Beck, who was the Dean of Men at BSTC prior
to enlisting in the Army Air Corps, serves at the Central Gunners
school at Fort Meyers, Florida, after completing the flexible gunnery
course at Buckingham Field. Captain Beck training men who will
instruct in gunnery schools and in overseas training units.

Seaman second class Harold T. Hagg joined the military leaving
his position at the BSTC as an instructor in the social studies division. When Hagg left for military duty, he was the acting chairman
of the division. Seaman Hagg is stationed currently (December 16,
1943) at the US Naval Construction Training Center at Camp Peary,
Virginia, where is works at the ship's company library.

---

[41] Uncredited, "Reasons to be Thankful," *The Northern Student*, November 24,
1943, 2.

[42] Richard Daggy, "Lieut. Daggy Speaks at College Tonight," *The Bemidji Daily
Pioneer*, December 14, 1943.

December of 1943 marked many activities themed around the Christmas holiday. The annual Christmas party was held on December 10 in the gymnasium. There were many decorated Christmas trees. There was a large tree in the center of the gymnasium, which the students circled and caroled. There was a Christmas message from President A. C. Clark, various readings and solo vocal performances. Punch and cookies were served from a decorated table, followed by social and folk dancing as well as games in a natural Christmas setting. On Friday morning, December 17, the students, and faculty gathered in the little theater for an hour of singing Christmas carols. Sunday evening, December 12 marked the evening whereupon the seventh annual Christmas concert was presented at the First Lutheran Church in the form of a Pageant on the Nativity. The presentation consisted of songs by the chorus and readings and themes from the Christmas story.

The eighth-grade laboratory students set a new high record in bond and stamp sales in December, raising a total of $4,425.40.

When asked what students and staff wanted for Christmas, many of their wishes were directly related to the conditions created by the war. "Santa, because you are so fortunate as to have reindeer with which to travel, you can't imagine the difficulty we have when gas is rationed. That is why several students are asking for 'C' books. Although no one has mentioned the fact, we believe the college girls would be very grateful if you would bring down at least part of the Navy Air Corps unit we have been hearing about. Or, please Santa, bring us some veterans. Our closing request echoes the thoughts of everyone in college. Miss Mabel Parker and Dr. Phillip Sauer ask for nothing more or less for Christmas than 'peace on earth, good will toward men.'"[43]

---

[43] Uncredited, *The Northern Student*, December 15, 1943, 2.

1944

1944 PROVED TO BE ONE of increased opportunity for the Bemidji State Teachers College students. Student health services were provided with new equipment (examination table, medicine cabinet, and an electrometric hemometer—used to measure hemoglobin content—the only one in Bemidji!) as well as additional course offerings as now speech minor was offered.

It was also noted in December that Pfc. *Robert Worth*, former student at BSTC, stationed at the University of Oregon, was then home on furlough. Robert had been taking courses in engineering in connection with the Army Specialized Training Program.

The college remained steadfast in its efforts to contribute to the war effort. The laboratory school students were still hard at work selling bonds and stamps, having reached a total of $4,641.35 by the middle of January. The student League of Women Voters conducted a waste-paper drive in which they collected about a ton and a half of waste-paper. The paper at that time was selling for between fifteen and twenty dollars a ton, depending on whether the paper was magazines, newspapers or corrugated paper. The BSTC girls were waiting to receive their quota for the production of surgical dressings and announced that during winter term the Red Cross room would be open Tuesdays and Thursdays from 3:00 p.m. to 6:00 p.m., and that between forty and fifty female students have signified that they would be helping. It was noted that during fall term one hundred and thirty-two students contributed and produced nearly 4000 bandages. The efforts of the volunteers did not go unnoticed. Dr. Hobson received a letter from PLM 2/c Ken Coder, which included an article about the number of surgical dressings made by the volunteers and had this to say, "This clipping from the paper can certainly be repeated again and again and in more than just our own paper too. It's one of the truest and best little items I've seen and should have been on the first page instead of the second. I'm in the hospital corps as you know, and we are never finished making bandages and compresses. It's a very continuous job, and we can't stop. We've been very fortunate to have our supplies replenished when we ran low. So believe me, all the 'bit' that is done soon grows and is used to the fullest extent. They're like fresh water—never wasted. The trimmings are saved and made into surgical sponges."[44]

The lack of male students on campus was not forgotten as marked by the comments posted in the student newspaper. "Get in Line Girls… There's a Man Loose Again"[45] as was also noted that for every male student there were six female students.

On Friday, February 11, 1944, the Alpha Phi Sigma Honorary Society presented at the regular assembly a Patriotic Program which included the reading of John Drinkwater's play, *Abraham Lincoln* by sophomore student Eva Cann.

February 1944 marked eighth-grade bond and stamp sales at over $8,000. The twofold goal was to, by the end of the first academic year, sell at least $5000 worth of bonds and stamps, and by the end of the second school year, achieve selling a bond for every lab school pupil. At the time of this report 37 percent of the lab school pupils had a bond apiece. This month also noted the creation of the Quill club (informally known as the ink-slingers) for those students interested in journalism and other creative writing. There was a poll given to students which asked if "The Star Spangled Banner" should be sung at the start of each school assembly and an overwhelming 80 percent yes by the students and 71 percent yes by the faculty ensured that, indeed, the anthem would be the start of each weekly school assembly. On a health note, it was reported that (as of February 23) only 30 percent of the student body had come down with the flu.

---

[44] Kenneth Coder, *The Northern Student*, February 23, 1944, 4.
[45] Uncredited, "Get in Line Girls… There's a Man Loose Again," *The Northern Student*, February 23, 1944, 3.

College clubs were in full swing with February meetings of the Rural Life club, Alpha Phi Sigma, the Sketch club, and the science club.

On an optimistic note, a questionnaire was sent out via the student paper to the men and women in military service regarding their choices and thoughts on post-war education.

The Northern Student, Wednesday, February 23, 1944, p. 3. (Bemidji State University Archives)

This is in conjunction with the plans being made by Congress to provide college education for ex-servicemen. Already in place through the veteran's bureau was assistance for disabled veterans who wished to pursue a college education and current bills were addressing items such as monthly allotments, expenses and tuition. BSTC, which is now a full accredited college, will be a college where education for ex-servicemen will be offered. The college had also recently voted to give credit to servicemen whose experience would relate to the subject matter being considered.

The student paper continued to lament the lack of male students and reportedly there was only one male student to every six female students, but it could have been worse as Moorhead college reported that there was one male student for every thirteen female students. Meanwhile, the faculty were busy at work for the Paul Bunyan district of the Boy Scouts by holding organizational meetings in the region and promoting the formation of troops. There were currently several troops in Bemidji and a newly formed troop in Blackduck.

Former student *John Shock* had written to Dr. Hobson and reported in the *Northern Student*:

> Shortly after I received your card we left the states. The Pacific indeed is terrific! There wasn't much to do aboard ship except to read, bathe in the sun and watch the mighty Pacific roll by day after day. Although for days there was nothing to look at but the sea and the sky, one never seems to tire of it. I've seen the waters of the Pacific in every color imaginable-including purple, with due credit to Miss Seeling! As an added thrill we were initiated into Neptune's Ancient Order of the Deep when we crossed the equator, for which we received membership cards. We crossed the International Date Line on a Sunday night, and an hour after midnight it was Tuesday morning. By the way, those who crossed the equator are dubbed Shellbacks; those who have not,

Pollywogs. About two days before we sighted land we ran into a typical South Sea hurricane without the Dorothy Lamour attached. But ours was a sturdy ship.

Of the South Pacific Island where Lt. Shock was stationed, he writes, "Our island is fairly large, inhabited by a muscular, dark-skinned, red-haired French-speaking native, who works for about thirty cents a day. A small village lies three miles from camp. There is no main thoroughfare in it, but a concourse of avenues lined with tiny shops and residents whose appearance reflect a dingy gray ancientness. It is often difficult to distinguish between shop and home. There are practically no recreation facilities for service men, so it is a poor liberty town. Being summer, the climate is mild. Of course, mosquitoes and ants are a constant pest while rain and hurricanes are a constant threat."

In conclusion, he says, "I should like to extend my sincere well-wishes to all my BSTC friends, both students and faculty alike. Lots of luck and success to Beaver athletic teams and the Northern Student too."[46]

Lt. Jim Lizer also writes from "somewhere," "Just now I am resting up from a tour of duty. A period of rest in Sydney, Australia is in the very near future, and that makes everything doubly fine. While up north, I flew off Vella la Vella and Bougainville. I saw Rabaul and had the satisfaction of paying back part of my debt to the government in the form of a Zero. I sincerely hope that you folks back home continue to give us all of the support you have in the past."

Howard Cords
Died in Service April 20, 1944

Howard Cords was a graduate of the Bemidji High School and then enrolled in the Bemidji State Teachers College, where he was prominent in athletics, later going on to the University of

---

[46] John Shock, *The Northern Student*, February 23, 1944, 4.

Minnesota. Howard Cords joined the Army Air Corps. Howard graduated from advanced flying school at Kelly Field, which is located not far from San Antonio, Texas, in 1940. Shortly thereafter he was sent to Hawaii and was there during the attack on Pearl Harbor on December 7, 1941. Captain Cords was awarded a combat medal for his actions taken that day. Based on news that was shared through Howard's family with the Bemidji Daily Pioneer it was noted that in July of 1942 the parents of then Captain Howard Cords had received a letter from Howard from an undisclosed location saying that he was serving as a controller in an information center and would be at his current location for several months. 1942 also marked the year that Howard became married to Cecile Jensen of Louisville, Kentucky, who then moved to New York City. In March of 1943, it was reported that Captain Cords had been promoted to Major and was stationed in Hawaii. Howard noted in his letter to his parents that he was planning on attending a "Minnesota party" the next day which was called the Minnesota Paul Bunyan Carnival, and he was hoping that he might run into someone he knew. Lastly, Howard noted that he was expecting to be sent on furlough shortly. In April of 1943, *The Bemidji Daily Pioneer* received a V-mail (V-mail was inaugurated by the US Postal Service in 1942 and was the preferred method of sending and receiving letters to and from servicemen. The written letter was microfilmed at the originating point for transportation overseas and then printed out for delivery at its destination station. This greatly reduced the weight of transporting written letters) from Major Cords reporting that he had attended the Paul Bunyan party and had met several people from the Minneapolis area but none from Bemidji.

(US Postal Service)

In July of 1943, *The Bemidji Daily Pioneer* reported that Major Cords had returned to the United States, and after picking up his wife in Boston, visited Bemidji, and that Major Cords had been serving with a fighter squadron in the Hawaiian Islands. Howard is reported to be staying in Bemidji while awaiting his next duty assignment.

In October of 1943, Major Cords had written to his parents from India, before being sent to China. As quoted in the Thursday Evening, February 10 edition of the *Bemidji Daily Pioneer*, Major Cords, who had just been transferred from India to China, writes,

> On the way over we had but one scare. While in India, we had an experience with a wild water buffalo, supposed to be the most dangerous animal alive to hunt. They are about twice the size of our domestic bulls, and twice as mean. There were 18 in the party. He charged us like an express train bearing down, but fortunately one of the boys put a bullet through his shoulder into his heart and

he stopped in his tracks. I probably won't be here writing this if he hadn't. The estimated weight was about 5.000 pounds, unbelievable I guess, but true according to the native guides. I also had an experience playing with a King Cobra, supposed to be the fiercest snake in India. Also was fortunate enough to have my picture taken with a python draped around my neck. Quite an experience! You might read about this particular route in Life magazine. Received quite a thrill when I first saw Mt. Everest, 29,300 feet in the air. The weather is like our fall. I am writing this with a pencil as ink is $5 a bottle here.[47]

Major Howard Cords. (*Bemidji Daily Pioneer*, Tuesday Evening, September 21, 1943. p. 3)

While in China, Major Cords was assigned to the Chinese-American Composite Wing. This joint designation signified that both American and Chinese pilots comprised the wing. All pilots

---

[47] Howard Cords, *The Bemidji Daily Pioneer*, February 10,1943.

assigned to the CACW were rated pilots in both the United States Army Air Corps as well as Chinese Air Force and were allowed to wear the pilot's wings of both countries. Major Cords was technically a part of the Eighth Fighter Squadron, which consisted of both fighter aircraft P-40 Warhawks and P-51 Mustangs. While stationed in China, Major Cords was assigned to fly the P-40N Warhawk. US personnel were assigned to the joint squadrons in mid-July of 1943. The P-40 Warhawks were marked with the National Chinese Air Force blue sky and twelve-pointed white sun national insignia, rudder markings and squadron/aircraft numbering while later assigned fighters, the P-51 Mustangs were marked with United States Army Air Force (USAAF) markings.

P-40N Warhawk in Chinese National Air Force markings. (Special Aircraft Service, June 2, 2016)

The CACW wing that Major Cords was assigned to was the Lingling base, which was located approximately nine kilometers for the city of Yangzhou, which is located in Hunan Province, China.

According to official USAAF records, on April 20, 1944, Major Cords was piloting a P-40N Warhawk, serial number 42-105919 when the aircraft crash landed at the Lingling air base, killing Major Cords. The aircraft was noted in the report as being so badly damaged that it was damaged beyond repair.

On May 2, 1944, the parents of Major Cords were notified of their son's death. *The Bemidji Daily Pioneer* noted the next day in the Wednesday edition of the paper that Major Cords also had a brother, Bob, who was serving in the military as well. Memorial services were held for Major Howard Cords on Sunday afternoon, May 14, 1944, at the Methodist church with the Reverend Crawford

Grays officiating. A large group of relative sand friends attended the rites. Howard is buried at the National Memorial Cemetery of the Pacific, Honolulu, Hawaii.

(National Memorial Cemetery of the Pacific, Honolulu, Hawaii.)

April of 1944 marked the annual start of the academic year's conclusion. The eighth-grade lab school students had sold close to $9000 worth of bonds and stamps and noted that the end of the drive would be May 2. The proceeds from the last two days of the drive, April 25 and May 2 would be used to sponsor a Garand rifle, which cost $75 each. It was announced that President Manfred Deputy (BSTC. President from 1918 to 1938) would be speaking at this year's Commencement. The Service Star flag, which was displayed outside the president's door, also has a list of the service men and women and where their star is located on the flag. The flag is kept up to date by the sewing efforts of the faculty wives. The call still went out for volunteers to make surgical dressings and emphasized that with the coming of an allied invasion of Europe (apparently not a big secret) the need for surgical dressings would be even greater. *Lt. Gilbert Lizer* had recently visited the college and had been in Puerto Rico and Trinidad as a member of the Army Air Corps. *Charles*

Marmorine and Garnette Nichols (both former BSTC students) were married on April 23 at the Methodist church. The questionnaire that had been sent to servicemen in February of 1943 showed, in general, chemistry was the most popular course to be offered post-war.

"From the replies received, the consensus of opinion is that international relations, foreign languages, chemistry and industrial arts will receive major emphasis after the war." One respondent replied, "In my estimation the burden of creating a lasting peace will fall on the educators." Every one of the respondents reported that they would be continuing their education.[48] April also saw the addition of seven cadet nurses taking a three-month rural sociology course. At the conclusion of that course, a new group of student nurses will arrive to take the same course. The Rural Life club was bust-sewing together afghans for the Red Cross while photography was the main topic of current interest with the Science club. The Women's Athletic Association (WAA) decided to add Kittenball as a new major sport. It will be played indoors until the weather is conducive to outdoor play. The college concluded its "Pin-Up" man for the spring. This event held a goal of raising $100 for the Red Cross. The female students were asked to submit photographs they had received by servicemen and a total of thirty-three photographs were submitted. These photographs were placed on two bulletin boards in the gymnasium lobby with a chart thermometer that recorded the progress of the drive. Votes were purchased by students for five cents each. The photograph with the most votes was declared the winner. This year's event raised a total of $109, surpassing the fund-raising goal. The winner was Seaman First Class James Seymour, stationed at Kodiak, Alaska, and submitted by Jackie Graham, freshman from Bethel, Kansas.

Former student Bob Hakkerup reported to the *Northern Student* that he had run into Lt. Jim Lizer. "*Jim Lizer* is now a Marine flier—though I haven't seen him out here I did bump into him in LA before I left California."[49]

---

[48] Uncredited, *The Northern Student*, April 26, 1944, 3.
[49] Bob Hakkerup, *The Northern Student*, April 26, 1944, 4.

Roger Hilstad
Killed in Action May 12, 1944

Roger Hilstad was born in Goodhue County, Minnesota, on March 14, 1922. Roger graduated from the Kenyon (Minnesota) High School in 1940 and then attended Bemidji State Teachers College. While attending Bemidji State Teachers College, Roger was a charter member of the BSTC Playmakers club in 1941. Roger attended BSTC for two years prior to entering the Army Air Forces. While staying in Bemidji to attend BSTC, Roger stayed with his aunt and uncle, Arnold and Mrs. Kindseth.

IN COLLEGE PLAY

"I told you everything would turn out happily!" says Sylvette, the heroine of Rostand's comedy, "The Romancers," which was performed for the assembly program on Feb. 14, by the college Drama club.

This "Romeo and Juliet" type of play was the first performance given by the newly formed college organization. The characters were George Lilliquist, Sylvette's father; Margaret Christie, Sylvette; Irvin Nordquist, Percinet; Roger Hilstad, Percinet's father; and Bruce Graves, the villain.

The Northern Student, February 28, 1941.
p. 1.(Bemidji State University Archives)

Roger received his pilot's wings on October 1, 1943, when he graduated from Moore Field, near Mission, Texas. Roger was then able to spend some time on furlough with his parents, in Kenyon, Minnesota.

Roger trained in the Army Air Corps to fly the P-51 Mustang fighter and left for England in January of 1943. Roger was eventually assigned to the 362 Fighter Squadron of the 357th Fighter Group, which was based out of Leiston, England, in February of 1943.

North American P-51 Fighter assigned to the 362 Fighter Squadron. (American Air Museum in Britain)

In the Monday Evening, May 29, 1944, of the *Bemidji Daily Pioneer*, it reported that information had been shared with them via the Kenyon Leader newspaper that Roger had been reported as being missing in action. The story reads, "Lieut. Roger A. Hilstad, son of Mr. and Mrs. Albert Hilstad of Kenyon, was reported missing in action in a telegram cleared through local Red Cross channels Monday of this week. The telegram inferred that Lieut. Hilstad failed to return to his home base in England following a mission over enemy territory on May 12. There is a possibility that the young flier may have parachuted to safety and is being held a prisoner of war, although no details were given in the telegram."[50]

Unfortunately, the news was not one of hope when it was reported in the *Bemidji Daily Pioneer* on March 13, 1945, "According

---

[50] Uncredited, *The Bemidji Daily Pioneer*, May 29, 1944.

to word received in Bemidji, Lieut. Roger A. Hilstad, son of Mr. and Mrs. Albert Hilstad of Kenyon, was reported killed in action in the European Area. Lt. Hilstad failed to return to his home base in England following a mission over European enemy territory May 12, 1944, his parents were informed thru red Cross channels."[51]

On May 12, Roger was assigned to be a part of a fighter escort for bombers over a mission to Czechoslovakia. The fatal air battle took place approximately twenty-three miles north of Wurzburg. In a statement by Capt. Maurice F. Baker, who was on the same mission that day, "I was the last person to see 2nd Lt. Roger A. Hilstad, 362nd FS, 357th FG. I last saw him about 23 miles north of Wurzburg, Czechoslovakia at 1245 hours on 12 May 1944. I was leading Dollar Squadron when, just after rendezvous, the front box of bombers was hit by ME-109s. Hilstad, my wingman and I went down after a formation of four of them. He was right behind me on my wing during the ensuing fight on the deck. I saw a ME-109 shoot at him, but he rolled out of the way away when I called for him to break. Apparently he had not been hit. Then I went after the ME-109 which had shot at my wingman and knocked him down. After this I looked around and didn't see Lt. Hilstad. I flew around, trying to find him and contact him by radio with no results."[52]

[51] Uncredited, "Lieut. Roger Hilstad Is Reported Killed," *The Bemidji Daily Pioneer*, March 13, 1945.

[52] Manuel F. Van Eyck, *Silent Heroes,* (Paducah, Kentucky: Turner Publishing, 2002).

Lt. Roger Albert Hilstad. (American Air Museum in Britain, http://www.americanairmuseum.com/media/26913)

Kenyon Cemetery. Kenyon, Goodhue County, Minnesota.

Walter Ervin Brotherton
Died in Service May 19, 1944

Walter Ervin Brotherton was born in Williams, Minnesota in 1922. At the time of his birth, his father, Henry Clyde Brotherton, was thirty-five years old and his mother, Mary Estella Jenks-Brotherton was thirty-two years of age. Walter had two older brothers, Glenn and Lee, and one older sister, Leta.

Walter was a clarinet player while a student at BSTC and represented the college at singing events outside of the college. It was noted in the *Northern Student* on November 28, 1941, that Walter was one of clarinet quintet that played at the Northwest Singers Annual Concert in Bagley, Minnesota. Another member of the quintet was student Harry Stoner, who was also to serve in the Pacific theater during WWII and died in a car crash near the Bemidji Golf Club very shortly after he returned from the service. Walter was one of the students who participated in the preliminary pilot Civilian Pilot Training program while a student at BSTC.

As reported in the Tuesday Evening, August 24, 1943, edition of the *Northern Student*, C. V. Hobson received a long distance call from his son, Rodney Hobson, who was serving in the military as an aviation cadet at the Jefferson Barracks, Missouri, along with Walter Brotherton and a number of former students who had taken CAA courses while students at BSTC.

While attending Bemidji State Teachers College, Walter registered for the draft on February 15, 1942.

(National Archives and Records Administration)

According to official military records, Aviation Cadet Brotherton had left his training base, at Corsicana Field, Texas flying a PT-19A trainer aircraft as the lone occupant.

PT-19A Military Trainer Aircraft. (Houston
Wing, Commemorative Air Force)

According to the Texas Death Certificate filed on Walter, here is what took place. At approximately 5:00 p.m. the afternoon of May 19, 1944, Cadet Brotherton was flying a PT-19A approximately five (5) miles southeast of Corsicana, Texas, when his aircraft went into a stall, which resulted in the aircraft going into a spin. Cadet Brotherton was unable to recover from the spin and crashed. Injuries sustained in the crash by Cadet Brotherton resulted in his death.

(United States War Department)

Funeral services were held for Walter Brotherton on Thursday afternoon, May 25, 1944, at the Pilgrim Congregational church at Williams, Minnesota, with the Reverend L. C. Neal, pastor of the Church of God at Roosevelt, Minnesota, officiating. Walter was buried at the Pine Hill Cemetery, Williams, (Lake of the Woods County) Minnesota.

James Lizer
Died in Service May 22, 1944

James Lizer was born on June 1, 1920, in Grand Rapids, Minnesota. James's mother passed away in 1937. James (Jim) became a student at BSTC and in the fall of 1941 was a multi-role player on the Beaver football team, officially listed as a kicker and punter but also, on occasion, played as a receiver, scoring at least one touchdown that season, as was noted in the September 29, 1941, edition of the *Northern Student*, "In regards to BSTC defeating Mayville State Teachers college, during the second quarter Otterstad again heaved a directly aimed pass to Jim Lizer in the end zone for the final tally." Jim was a member of the football, basketball, and track teams.

In January of 1942, Jim left BSTC for his training in the US Naval Air Corps. Prior to enlisting for Naval flight training, Jim had over 500 hours of flight time, ferrying tourists in a float plane to area lakes. In August of 1942, Jim and Harry Stoner Jr. (another former BSTC student) were being transferred from Wold-Chamberlin Field, where they had been taking preliminary Naval pilot training since June 4. Jim and Harry were being sent to the Navy base at Corpus Christi, Florida, for advanced training and expected to be commissioned Ensigns in another four and one-half months.

Cadet Lizer excelled as a cadet while stationed at Corpus Christi. Jim sent a letter to the *Bemidji Daily Pioneer* which included a newspaper clipping which read as follows, "Enclosed in a letter received from James Lizer recently was a newspaper clipping which reads as follows: 'Two new records were established on the obstacle course during the past week. Cadet J. W. Lizer of the 6th battalion scampered over the course in 2 minutes and forty-five seconds to establish a new record for the cadets.'"[53]

Jim Lizer graduated from the Naval Air Station at Corpus Christi, Texas, in August of 1942 and was commissioned as an Ensign in the United States Naval Reserve.

Ensign Lizer was given the option of serving as a pilot in the United States Marine Corps and he elected to do so. Thus Ensign Lizer became First Lieutenant Lizer, USMC Reserves. Lieutenant Lizer was then stationed in San Diego, California. During his leaves, Jim would visit his parents and friends in Bemidji.

---

[53] Uncredited, *The Bemidji Daily Pioneer*, August 31, 1942.

Lieutenant James Lizer. (Sgt. Bellis. USMC:
Find A Grave Member#48526889)

Lieutenant Lizer was eventually assigned to the Marine Attack Squadron VMF 223. VMF 223 was stationed in November of 1943 at Barokoma Field, Vella Lavella Island, Solomon Islands. Lieutenant Lizer and the pilots of VMF 223 were assigned the F4U Corsair.

F4U Corsair Assigned to VMF 223, Solomon Islands, 1943

The March 3, 1944, Friday Evening edition of the *Bemidji Daily Pioneer* headline read,

LIEUT. JIM LIZER DOWNS ZERO PLANE

> A news dispatch from Vella Lavella, Solomon Islands, says that Marine 1st Lt. James W. Lizer, 23, has a Jap Zero to his credit. He spotted the Zeros as his squadron flew over the harbor at Rabaul, New Britain. "It was coming at me head-on," he related. "I let him have it. The bullets blew the cockpit away and set him on fire. The Zero plummeted downward."[54]

While Lt. Lizer had success in the air, it was a hard time for the marine squadron. The Japanese pilots were becoming used to the aerial capabilities of the American aircraft and thus more deadly. The pilots of VMF 223 were busy the first half of 1944 flying escort, rescue-cover and strafing missions. The period from May 12 to June 16 was especially tragic for VMF 223 as they lost five pilots during those few short months.

James' father, Gilbert Lizer, Sr., passed away in 1943, while James was in service.

Lieutenant Lizer was one of those pilots lost in battle on May 22, 1944.

On June 15, 1944, *The Bemidji Pioneer* reported on the death of Lieutenant Lizer.

> Mrs. H. E. Stoner received a letter Wednesday from Mike Chilson for the boys of V-223 Squadron of Marines in the South Pacific, giving details of the recent death of Lieut. Jim Lizer who was killed in action, May 22nd. Chilson stated

---

[54] Uncredited, "Lieut. Lizer Downs Zero Plane," *The Bemidji Daily Pioneer*, March 3. 1944.

that they were returning from a hop when Lizer sighted an enemy barge just off shore and went down alone to strafe it, and the Jap shore batteries caught him with terrific cross fire and he dived into the water where the plane exploded. All his men went down to rescue him, but the body was not found. Mr. Chilton said all the boys in the division thought a lot of Jim and of his high ideals and mentioned that he held the group spell-bound when he was telling them about Bemidji."[55]

Upon the death of Lieutenant Lizer, there was a special Invasion Day Prayer Services for Lizer held at the Methodist church. Lt. Lizer had, just prior to his death, been awarded a medal for extraordinary bravery in the line of duty.

The official status of Lieutenant Lizer is "missing" while his headstone is located at the Manila American Cemetery and Memorial, Manila, Capital District, National Capital Region, Philippines.

Archie D. Graves
Died in Service May 27, 1944

Archie Graves was born at Red Lake, Minnesota on May 11, 1918. Archie graduated from the Red Lake High School and then became a student at the Bemidji State Teachers College from the fall quarter of 1937 until his graduation in the spring of 1939 with a two-year standard diploma that was issued on June 6, 1939. Archie and his brother, Bryon, were noted as being the first American Indian students at BSTC.

---

[55] Uncredited, "Details Received on Death of Lieut. Lizer," *The Bemidji Pioneer*, June 15, 1944, 1.

(*The Ashkabewis*. 1977–1978 edition. p. 3)

Archie was noted to have been prominent in his science work while a student at BSTC. At that time, the two-year diploma led to a teaching certificate. After graduation, Archie took a teaching position in Guthrie, Minnesota. At the age of twenty-two, Archie registered with the draft and listed his employer as the Red Lake Indian Agency. On March 27, 1941, Archie enlisted in the Army Air Corps at the recruitment office located at Fort Snelling. Archie completed is primary training at Muskogee, Oklahoma, at the Third Army Air Force, 349th Army Air Forces Base Unit, which is now known as the Muskogee-Davis municipal airfield.

In November of 1943, Archie married Florence Lee at the home of Reverend W. K. Boyle of Bemidji while on leave from Camp Carlsbad, New Mexico, as an instructor. The wedding was witnessed by immediate family and friends.[56]

After Archie completed his training with the Army Air Corps, he was assigned as a sergeant. Archie Graves was assigned to the 410th Bomb Group, which was part of the Ninth Air Force.

Archie was able to make a visit home during his time in service and prior to being sent overseas. This is believed to be one of the last family photographs taken with the Graves family when Archie was home on leave prior to being sent to England.

(Photograph courtesy of Eloise Graves-Jallin)

The 410th Bomb Group was sent to England from the United States during the months of March and April of 1944. The 410th Bomb Group flew the Boston A-20 Havoc and was stationed out of the Gosfield Air Base, which was located northeast of London, England. The 410th Bomb Group as part of the Ninth Air Force, entered combat in May of 1944. The typical crew for the A-20 con-

---

[56] Uncredited, "Society News," *The Bemidji Daily Pioneer*, November 7, 1943, 2.

sisted of a pilot, navigator, and gunner. It is unclear which position Archie was assigned (either navigator or gunner).

Boston A-20 "Havoc" of the 410th Bomb Group.
(American Air Museum in Britain)

Prior to leaving the east coast for England, Archie had the opportunity to eat at one of the most popular bar and restaurants in New York City, Jack Dempsey's Broadway Bar, and sent these photos home to his family.

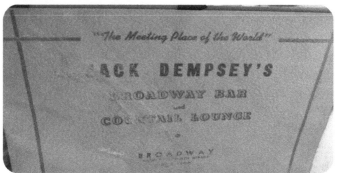

(Photographs courtesy of the Eloise Graves-Jallin)

On May 27, 1944, Sergeant Archie Graves was a crewmember of an A-20-G havoc (aircraft serial number 43-9965) that left Gosfield Air Base on a mission to bomb a target in Amiens, France, which is in northern France, south of the Belgium border.

According to the Army Air Corps Missing Air Crew Report (MACR), the A-20 Havoc that was manned by Sgt. Archie Graves (there is some discrepancy in that there are conflicting records as to Archie's official rank, as some sources state his rank as Private and the MACR listed Archie's rank as Sergeant), piloted by 2nd Lieutenant Raymond L. Gregg, who incidentally was on loan from the Royal Canadian Air Force, and Sergeant Budd W. Teare. At approximately

1:30 p.m., the aircraft was approximately forty-six miles southwest of their intended target (the records do not indicate if the flight was returning from the target zone or approaching) when the aircraft was hit by an enemy flak. The aircraft crashed approximately four miles north of Forge Les Eaux, France. Immediately after the crash, people (the report does not say if it was local citizenry or German military personnel) approached the aircraft, which had been on fire, and found all three crewmen deceased. The pilot, Lieutenant Gregg, had been thrown from the aircraft while Archie and Budd were found still in the aircraft. The aircrew was then buried in the local French cemetery located at Poix. Archie Graves has a memorial gravesite located at the Fort Snelling National Cemetery.

Cemetery located at Poix, France. (aircrewremembered.
com/james-ernest.html)

In the June issue of the *Northern Student* it was noted that the final tally for surgical dressings made by BSTC students fall, and spring quarters was 8, 143. Two hundred ninety-five volunteers spent 520 hours volunteering to make the bandages. The top volunteer was Laura Shogren, who volunteered eighteen and a quarter hours. President Emeritus Manfred Deputy visited the campus and was quoted as stating. "I am very proud of the fine spirit among the students and faculty; it is a continuation of the same spirit that existed as I remember the school."[57] June of 1944 also marked the graduation of fifty-two students—twenty-four four-year students and twenty-eight two-year students comprised the graduating class. Senior skip day that year was held at the Itasca State Park.

July 21, 1944, would prove to be the single deadliest day for the student soldiers of the Bemidji State Teachers College. This day would be eternally saddened with the deaths of two former students, Kenneth Gregg and John Shock.

Kenneth Gregg
Killed in Action July 21, 1944

Kenneth Gregg was born in Tenstrike, Minnesota, on August 14, 1922. Kenneth enrolled at the Bemidji State Teachers College in the fall of 1940. Kenneth registered for the draft in Bemidji on June 30, 1942, and at that time, was residing at 401 Park Avenue, Bemidji. On June 30, 1942, Kenneth registered for military service in Bemidji and his physical description on his registration card listed Kenneth as being 5'4" tall, weighing 141 pounds. It could be safely assumed that Kenneth was a popular student at the college, as shortly after he left the college for military service this was noted in the student paper, "The college lost one good man, however short on size, when Kenny Gregg left for the Army Air Corps, a couple weeks back. To compensate, however, Walt Brotherton has returned to take primary CPT training."[58]

---

[57] Uncredited, *The Northern Student*, June 7, 1944, 1.
[58] Uncredited, *The Northern Student*, January 27, 1943, 2.

REGISTRATION CARD—(Men born on or after January 1, 1922 and on or before June 30, 1924)

(National Archives)

After his basic training, Kenneth was stationed at the Army Air base in Santa Anna, California, for two weeks of preliminary tests and training before starting a nine-week schooling course. In February, Kenneth earned his pilots' wings, and in April, Kenneth completed his preflight training and was transferred to Twentynine Palms, California, to take advanced training. After completing the training at Twentynine Palms, Kenneth was transferred to the Army Air Corps Airfield located in Stockton, California. While stationed at Stockton Field, Kenneth married June Plavan on October 13, 1944. Kenneth graduated as a pilot and gained the rank of lieutenant on Wednesday, November 3, 1944.

Shortly after graduation from the advanced training at the Stockton Airfield, Kenneth was transferred to the four-engine (bomber) training airfield located at the Hobbs Army Airfield, New Mexico. Kenneth was transferred to the Kearney Army Air Base at Kearney, Nebraska, and while there in May of 1945, learned that he was to soon be sent overseas. His wife was to move back to her home town of Santa Ana, California, once Kenneth left for Europe.

By the middle of June 1945, Kenneth had arrived in England and was stationed at the Rougham Air Field, which was located northeast of London. Kenneth's parents received a letter from him in June and Kenneth stated that he liked England and that the scenery reminded him of Minnesota.

Rougham airfield was constructed in 1942 and covered 250 acres and was located approximately three miles east of Bury St. Edmunds, Suffolk, England. Rougham airfield had three intersecting concrete runways, the longest being 2,000 feet long. The Rougham Ninety-Fourth Bombardment Group (Heavy) arrived at Rougham Field on June 15, 1943. The Ninety-Fourth consisted of B-17 "Flying Fortresses," and their group tail code was the "Square-A."

THE ALLEN CREW

Kenneth Gregg, Top Row first on the left.
(United States Army Air Corps Photo)

B-17 Flying Fortress of the Ninety-Fourth Bombardment Group. (Photograph courtesy of the Rougham Control Tower Aviation Museum. https://rctam94[th].co.uk/history)

The Rougham Airfield Traffic Control Tower. (Britain American Air Museum https://www.americanairmuseum.com/media/15141)

On July 21, 1944, Lt. Gregg was assigned as the pilot of B-17 # 42-31013 "Myassam Dragon" on a bombing mission to Regensburg, Germany. According to the Army Air Corps Missing Aircraft Report (MACR)# 7836, "This aircraft was hit by flak on course into target at 51°20'N–04°40'E while flying at 20000 feet at 0850 hours. Aircraft appeared to be hit between #1 and #2 engine. Aircraft turned over on its back and then resumed normal flying position. It then dropped off into a spin and was seen to explode before hitting the ground.

Aircraft was burning and the flames were visible. Four (4) chutes were observed. No further information regarding the crew or aircraft is known." The crash occurred near Bavel, Holland, and none of the crew was ever seen alive after the crash.

"Myassam Dragon" Unidentified Crewman. (Army Air Corps)

On August 8, 1944, Kenneth's parents were notified that Kenneth was officially reported as being Missing in Action (MIA). In January of 1945, Kenneth was awarded the Air Medal, and there was still hope that Kenneth had been taken a prisoner of war.

In February of 1945, Kenneth was officially listed as killed in action. Kenneth had only been stationed in England for two months prior to being shot down. Kenneth was survived by his parents, siblings, and wife, who was then residing in Santa Ana, California.

FIRST LT. KENNETH GREGG,
23, son of Mrs. June Plavan
Gregg, Rt. 4, Box 246, Santa
Ana, was shot down over Belgium July 21, 1944.

Erroneous information on the photograph caption: This should
have read, "Husband of June Plavan Gregg." (Photo added to
"Find A Grave" site for Kenneth Gregg by Charles Lewis Beal)

Kenneth's body was later recovered (the circumstances unavail-
able), and in 1949, his body was brought back to the United States
and buried at the Fort Snelling National Cemetery, located in
Minneapolis, Minnesota.

(United States Veterans Affairs Office Archives)

John Savo Shock
Died in Service July 21, 1944

John Shock, known as Johnnie, was from Nashwauk, Minnesota, and was very active as a student at the Bemidji State Teachers College. Johnnie was an amateur boxer and would volunteer to participate in benefit fights to raise money for various causes. Johnnie was noted to have won a close decision on a benefit fight card on January 22, 1941, over Russ Merritt of Hackensack, at the Bemidji National Guard Armory.

During the 1940–1941 academic year Johnnie acted the sports editor and college athletic publicity manager. In October of 1941, Johnnie was selected to be the co-editor of the *Northern Student*, along with Ralph Sorvig of Crookston.

Coeds Give Award To Co-Eds

—Courtesy of Duluth Herald News Service

Coeds Ruth Ellingson and Verna Barr, last year's editors, present the All-American award won by last year's Northern Student staff to the new co-editors Ralph Sorvig and John Shock.

The Northern Student, Monday, October 27, 1941, Volume XV. p. 1. (Bemidji State University Archives)

An interesting item to note regarding the student newspaper is that a letter, a "B" with a scroll, is to be awarded to those student reporters who contributed a minimum average of ten column inches per issue. A pin for the letter was awarded for two years' work, and a guard for the pin was awarded for three years' work. And for the first time, an award would be given for four years of work. At the time of this report, the fourth year award was not described.

There was a growing sentiment that the United States should not feel that they are immune from the war in Europe. As Gideon Seymour, chief editorial staff writer of the *Minneapolis Star Journal* and former head of the Associated Press in London, stated at an assembly held at the Bemidji State Teachers College on Friday, October 10, 1941, "We have been taught too long that as long as Britain is holding her place in the world, we are relatively safe…as long as there is any danger out of Europe in any direction—we aren't safe until Hitler is overthrown."[59]

---

[59] Gideon Seymour, "US Not Safe from War," *The Northern Student*, Volume XV, October 27, 1941, 1.

New Members of Who's Who

"Selected on the basis of character, leadership, scholarship and potentialities, nine students of the Bemidji State Teachers College were named in this year's edition of 'Who's Who in American Colleges and Universities.' Six (John Shock) were selected for the first time. Johnnie Shock, Nashwauk, is co-editor of the *Northern Student*, secretary of the student council, treasurer of the 'B' club, and member of the football squad." Johnnie was very engaged while a student at the BSTC and was recognized for his outstanding character and achievements.

∴ New Members of Who's Who ∴

Reading left to right: Paula Bruss, Herbert Fisher, Dorothy Setterholm, John Shock, Rachel Peterson and Wade Davis.

The Northern Student. Friday, November 28, 1941.
(Bemidji State University Archives)

It was evident by the way Johnnie kept in touch with the students and faculty at BSTC after he had enlisted that he felt a close relationship with the college. A letter that he had written to Dr. Phillip Sauer the first half of April 1943, was shared with the college through the *Northern Student* in their section of the paper entitled, "Thus Writes the Warrior."

> Recently Dr. Phillip Sauer received the following word from Corporal John Shock, 1942 graduate. Golden Gloves champion, English major, former sports editor, leatherneck: "I was happy to get your card and the journalism pin. The fine journalism

pin immediately brought back, and will continue to bring back, fond memories in association with the Northern Student. I feel so proud to have been on the staff of such a fine college paper for two years. It was indeed a grand pleasure to get the last issue of the *Northern Student*. I enjoyed every word of it. 'It's Shocking' how much I enjoy 'it's A'Maesing.' 'Thus Writes the Warrior' is extremely good. So is Mona Hoganson's 'Just Comment.' "Quotes from Quale'? Well, I read it. Tsk! Tsk! I can sincerely say that every bit of information regarding college and college activities is appreciated a hundred-fold—more after you've gone. As for my career in the Marines, it hasn't been nearly as exciting as I expected it to be; but of course, the near future is prospective. I've been 'standing by' for OC school for a long time-too long it seems. It's spring here now and the low. Rolling mountain ranges are covered with a verdant carpet of grass and green foliage. Instead of lakes and streams the mighty blue Pacific assumes a proud and majestic air of royalty. We had a four-minute earthquake in October to offset California's good points."[60]

Johnnie was listed in the *Northern Student*, June 8, 1943, Honor Roll of Our Servicemen at this location.

Pfc. John Shock
MCS Company H
26th Candidate Class MCS
Marine Barracks
Quantico, Virginia

---

[60] John Shock, Letter to Professor Sauer, *The Northern Student*, April 13, 1943, 3.

As a student teacher in the laboratory school, Johnnie was remembered with fondness. One of the former pupils at the laboratory school at that time, Pat Beaumont, remembers Johnnie as being very well liked. Pat shared her lab school experience with me in this email.

I was privileged to be chosen to attend the training school for student teachers called Lab School. It was a selected and limited class chosen from all economic classes in the area of Bemidji and the surrounding rural area. Of course all faculty children were automatically enrolled. Also, once a family member was accepted the whole rest of the siblings were too. My time there went from 1932 to 1943 and my Bender siblings all attended.

There were Master Teachers at each level that mentored and supervised all the student teachers. My unique situation was to be in Junior High during THE WAR. Master Teachers were Harry Bucklin (7th) Gordon M A MORK (8th), who later on became the head of the U of M Education Dept and was knighted by the King of Norway. Probably my best teacher of all time. Miss Frances McKee was 9th grade. They were all great patriots that instilled in us a love of country. We repeated The Pledge of Allegiance and shared Current events each morning. We bought war stamps and saved to buy Bonds, contributed to the Red Cross, collected scrap for the drives, and were encouraged to get pen pals from a list they had of children from Allied countries and soldiers. We were also asked to try to grow VICTORY GARDENS to alleviate the food shortage and some that was rationed.

Undoubtedly the most unique course we took was one from Dr. Mork that was about learning to identify airplanes from their silhouettes! Both US and Axis planes included. How could I forget B24, B17, Zero and Messerschmitt AMONG OTHERS. It was a difficult course but fun.

By the 9th grade we lost one of our friends as her father moved the family to Florida, Laredo Texas and then Hawaii. He was professor E W BECK and because he had served in the primitive Army Air Corps in WW1, he was called back. Another of the faculty kids, Norma Jean High, did graduate 9th grade with us but her father, Professor Marathon High (36 YRS) was called, by the Navy, to teach cadets math at Princeton U in New Jersey. Both men returned for a while to BSTC but moved on to Kansas City and Georgia as they thought BSTC was not going to last.

We were aware, as was everyone else, of all the restrictions that we should obey and contribute to the WAR EFFORT. Shoes were rationed, as was food that required coupons to buy, as well as butter. Gasoline rationing made unnecessary trips impossible as well as the inability to purchase no new tires at all. Like John Shock said in his letter "This is WAR). We were certainly aware and trying to do our part.

Despite all, we had a graduation from 9th grade and prepared to enroll at Bemidji High in the Fall. There were limited activities there, too, because of the war. However, most of the Lab. school kids were leaders because of all the extras they had been exposed to in Lab School. I was proud to have been trained there!" (Pat Beaumont recollection April 19, 2021)

Pat also shared a letter that Johnnie had written to her when he was serving in the Marines. This letter dated June 26, 1943, shared some of Johnnie's thoughts.

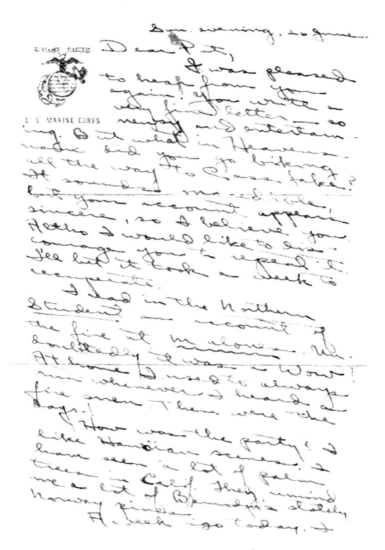

Letter to then Laboratory School student Pat Beaumont,
June 26, 1943. (Courtesy of Pat Beaumont)

Lt. John Shock's Death Reported

Word that Lt. John Shock was killed in action
on Guam, July 21, was recently received from
the war department. Lt. Shock of Nashwauk,
Minn., enlisted with the Marines in 1942 shortly

after his graduation from BSTC. At college he was exceptionally versatile and participated in nearly every type of activity offered. He was president of the "B" club, editor and sports editor of the Northern Student, secretary of the student council, was elected to Who's Who in American Colleges in the fall of 1941, a graduate of the C.A.A. flying course, and was a member of various musical organizations. He was a track and football letterman and won a trophy in the Northwest Collegiate Boxing championship at Superior in 1941. He also participated in a number of Golden Glove tournaments. Lt. Shock had majors in English and Social Studies and a minor in physical education. Typical of him is the statement he made in answer to, "What would you most like to be doing ten or fifteen years from now?" He said, "In a position helping other people."[61]

Johnnie's death, which included the details of his death were written in the *Bemidji Daily Pioneer* on Monday evening, September 10, 1944.

Road Named for College Athlete

A news clipping telling how the memory of Nashwauk officer and a former BSTC athlete has been honored, was received by Bemidji friends from Mr. and Mrs. Sava Shock, Nashwauk, parents of the marine. The news story says:

Paying high tribute to a gallant marine, Lieut. John S. Shock of Nashwauk, the First Battalion

---

[61] Uncredited, "Lt. John Shock's Death Reported," *The Northern Student*, October 20, 1944, 4.

of the Third Marine division recently dedicated a road within the base camp area to the memory of the young officer. Major General G. B. Erskine wrote to Mr. and Mrs. Shock: "I am enclosing a photograph of a road within our base camp area which was recently dedicated to the memory of your son, as a mark of the admiration and respect felt for him by his own comrades. I can pay this gallant marine no higher tribute than to echo the words of the order naming the road, a copy of which I will send you. Your son's name will not be forgotten and his devotion to duty and brave spirit will be an inspiration and example to all of us in the hard battles which still lie ahead."

In the order naming the street in honor of Lieut. Shock, the executive officer of his unit stated that Lieut. Shock's performance of duty as platoon leader of B company was at all times excellent.

"Lieut. Shock participated in the assault phase of the occupation of enemy-held Guam, Marianas Island. While leading his platoon against heavy enemy small arms fire on the morning of July 21, 1944, Lieut. Shock was killed by enemy fire. His performance of duty and his outstanding leadership were a constant source of inspiration to his men. His conduct was at all times in keeping with the high standards of the US naval service. The Nashwauk serviceman, who was 23 when he was killed in action, was a graduate of Nashwauk high school, Hibbing Junior college, and the State Teachers College at

Bemidji in 1942. He was outstanding in athletics during his school career."[62]

Johnnie was interred at the Maple Hill Cemetery in Hibbing, Minnesota.

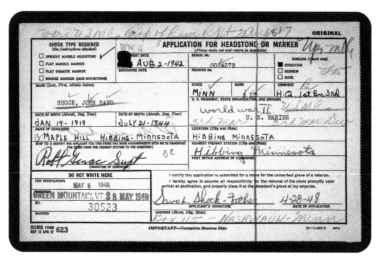

(United States Veterans Affairs Office Archives)

* * * * *

Fall of 1944 noted that students were asking for a student lounge. The argument being one of stairways being clogged by students hanging around to socialize and thus creating a potential hazard as well as inconvenience. Currently, the library was being used to gather, but that was not optimal as it is a place for study. This has been an ongoing issue at the school, and while there exists faculty support, nothing seems to be moving forward. The administration committee unanimously passed a motion the past March 3 favoring the opening of a student lounge.

---

[62] G. B. Erskine, Letter to the Parents of John Shock, *The Northern Student*, October 20, 1944, 4.

The student paper also promoted bond and stamp sales, noting that during the last academic year there was $9,187 worth of bonds and stamps sold. The article entitled, "Forego That Coke And Save a Life… Buy Those Bonds," noted that a $25 bond would buy a field telephone, a complete tropical uniform, or 104 rounds of .50 caliber ammunition. The eight grade laboratory school students would once again be selling the bonds and stamps.

BSTC was adamantly in favor of the new GI Bill of Rights, whereupon any serviceman who became vocationally handicapped since entering the service in September 16, 1940, would be entitled to vocational rehabilitation. Those eligible would be granted up to four years of vocational training, the government picking up the tab for tuition, books, supplies, and equipment, plus providing $92 a month maintenance and more, if married. The veteran will be able to choose which type of training best suits him, and the only condition is that the veteran be eligible for hiring once the training is complete. For those veterans who were not vocationally disabled the government (providing he served ninety days or more) would provide one year of further education if not over twenty-five years old when he entered the service or can prove that his education was disrupted by his service. After the first successful year of education, the veteran would then be entitled to additional education not to exceed the length of time he was in the service. The government would pay up to $500 in tuition costs plus fees and supplies and provide a subsistence allowance of $50 a month if there are no dependents or $75 a month with dependents. Applications for such aid, in either case, must be made within two years of the veteran's discharge date.

As has been the case since the start of the war, the female student body continued to lament the lack of male students.

Hail The Conquering Heroes

Shown in the above picture are six BSTC co-eds obviously very much interested in two young men, both of whom are veterans. The admiring young ladies are, left to right, Pauline Alich, Eleanor Anderson, Doris Van Winkle, Lois Baney, Jackie Graham and Ruth Austin.

The veterans, Millard Forsythe, left, and Everett White, right, both enrolled at BSTC this fall. Forsythe, who has had considerable experience as a flyer in the Navy Air corps, was given a medical discharge in July. White, who was in the Army Air corps, received a medical discharge in October, 1943, but remained in Washington for some time, where he did statistical work for the War Department. Both men are receiving compensation from the government and are applying it on their education.

The Northern Student, Wednesday, Sept. 27, 1944, p. 3. (Bemidji State University Archives)

Plans were in progress for the annual Beaver Day celebration, scheduled for the week of October 13. The week's festivities included a bonfire, Pepfest and snake dance, queen coronation, football game (this year against Eau Claire Teachers College), and immediately following the football game, there will be a flag-raising ceremony during which the ex-servicemen at the college will be honored.

Captain C. R. Sattgast was now in Europe and was stationed in France. Captain Sattgast's current station was formerly a German Nazi headquarters. Captain Sattgast noted to letters to his wife, the condition of the facility was left in a hurry and was in extreme disarray and unsanitary. Captain Sattgast presented an American flag to the mayor of a liberated French city.

A scene during the liberation of France. Captain C.R. Sattgast (upper left, holding flag) of the Allied Military Government is presenting an American flag to the mayor of a French city which has been liberated by the Americans. In the foreground is a Canadian band playing "The Star-Spangled Banner."

The Northern Student, Friday, October 20, 1944, p. 1. (Bemidji State University Archives)

The continuing human cost of war was ever-present at the college. An article in the October 20 edition of the *Northern Student* recognized that cost.

For Those Who Gave Their All… Eight Gold Stars

The Bemidji State Teachers College keeps a service record of all students and professors who have enlisted or been called into military service from the college since September 1940. Former alumni, students and professors are not included in this record. The roster includes 360 servicemen at the present time. Each serviceman is represented by a blue star on the service banner hanging in the gymnasium. Eight of these blue stars have been replaced by gold ones in memory of those who have died in the service of their country. Memorial trees have also been planted on the campus for each of the former students.

Lieutenant John Shock of Nashwauk was reported killed in action on Guam, July 21, 1944. He had been overseas with the United States Marine Corps since December of 1943.

Word was received June 9, 1944, that Lieutenant James Lizer of Litchfield, United States Marine Corps, had been killed in action near Rabaul in the South Pacific. He had been awarded a medal for extraordinary bravery in the line of duty and had at least one Japanese Zero to his credit.

Aviation cadet Walter Brotherton of Williams was fatally injured in a plane crash May 19th, 1944, near Milford, Texas.

Memorial services were held March 17, 1944, for Lieutenant John McCormick of Bemidji who was reported missing on an operational flight in the western European area February 16, 1943. He was awarded the Air Medal and the Purple Heart.

Lieutenant Harry Roese Jr. of Bemidji was killed in action on August 25, 1943, while flying the Burma Road patrol. He had been decorated with the Distinguished Flying Cross and the Air Medal and had been recommended for the China Flying Cloud decoration.

In June 1943, an official report was received of the death of Robert McPartlin, of St. Paul who had been reported missing in action over the African desert since September 9, 1942. He had served as navigator of his plane and was awarded the Purple Heart.

Ensign Edgar Arnold of Bagley was killed
in a crash of a naval patrol plane as it was taking
off on a routine flight on January 18, 1943, near
Elizabeth, North Carolina.

Second Lieutenant Malcolm Getchell of St.
Paul was killed in the crash of an Army bomber
near Richburg, South Carolina, on October 14,
1942.[63]

October of 1944 brought the introduction of the War Service
Fund drive to the campus. This new fund is now a part of the
National War Fund and monies raised will go toward USOs (United
Service Organizations), War Prisoners' Aid, and other agencies of
relief. The 1944 drive is aimed at also continuing these services after
the war is over. Faculty, students, and staff are encouraged to contribute. As a show of support, all were encouraged to wear the fund
drive lapel pin. As always, students were asked to attend Red Cross
surgical dressings. These meetings were being held several nights a
week downtown in the Dickenson building, as well as several meetings being scheduled in the BSTC gymnasium. The student lounge,
which was long sought after by the students was becoming a real-
ity. The cafeteria was the chosen location and $300 had been allo-
cated for the purchase of furniture if there was not enough furniture
donated. The students were asked to look for any furniture that was
serviceable. Furniture needing a coat of paint, or a little upholstering
was certainly welcome. This month also welcomed the Queen of the
Homecoming week, Marjorie Spilde, who was the first two-year student to be selected as queen. Marjorie was from Halma, Minnesota.

---

[63] Uncredited, "For Those Who Gave Their All… Eight Gold Stars, *The Northern
Student*, October 20, 1944, 2.

Willard (Bill) O. Johnson
Died in Service October 27, 1944

Willard (Bill) Owen Johnson was born on May 21,1921 and was the oldest of five sons of Alfred and Emma Johnson, of Sebeka, Minnesota. Living relatives told the author that Bill was always an adventurous type and was well liked. Unfortunately, there were no official records to be found of Willard's academics while attending the Bemidji State Teachers College.

Once Bill became a student at BSTC, he remained involved in football, basketball, and track as his physical stature was surely an asset (at Bill's time of enlistment he was recorded as being 6'2" in height and weighing 170 pounds). Bill enlisted in the Army Air Force (AAF) in Bemidji on February 10, 1941.

Willard (Bill) was one of seven brothers of the same family who served in the military during WWII from Sebeka, Minnesota.

(Courtesy of the Wadena County-Minnesota Historical Society)

In June of 1942, Bill reported to Minter Field, California, to begin his basic training as an aviation cadet in the Army Air Force. As part of his training at Minter Field, Bill would take ground school, then formation flying, and cross-country flying. Bill was listed on the Northern Student's Honor Roll of Our Servicemen in June of 1943.

Bill trained as a B-25 "Mitchell" bomber pilot and was assigned to the 490th Bomb Squadron. As part of that squadron, he was stationed at Guadalcanal and other Southwest Pacific locations.

Willard Johnson receiving commendation (unknown
location). (Photo by Daniel Bon)

Bill was listed on the Honor Roll of Servicemen in the June 8, 1943, edition of the *Northern Student*.

Bill was later assigned to the Burma theater of operations and was part of the 490th Army Air Force Bomb Squadron, the "Burma Bridge Busters." The squadrons mission at that time was to destroy bridges in territory held by the Japanese, which would then disrupt their supply lines and cause military operations to become more difficult.

B-25 Mitchell of the 490th Bomb Squadron (Note Skull with
Wings squadron logo). Rhode Island Aviation Hall of Fame.
https://riahof.org/news/2019-honorees-announced

On October 27, 1944, Bill was to pilot a B-25 Mitchell on a mission classified as "bomb-strafe-recon" from an airfield in the state of Assam, India. Bill was the pilot of B-25 serial number 43-4382 and left the airfield at 11:42 a.m. in good weather, with other bombers of his group that day. Their destination that day was the Luskia Road bridge in what was then Burma. When the group of B-25s reached their target, Bill's aircraft approached the target at a low altitude, and tragically, the aircraft was struck and damaged by a bomb that had been released from one the B-25s that was flying at a higher altitude. When the bomb was dropped to the ground, it was at the precise moment when Bill's aircraft was passing at low altitude directly over it. The explosion fatally damaged the aircraft, and it crashed shortly after the explosion. All five crewmen were killed.

As reported in an after-action report filed by fellow pilot First Lieutenant Herbert Schwarz regarding the aircraft piloted by Willard in aircraft number 4382,

> While circling the target area at Lashio I watched a B-25 as it made its bomb run on the bridge. A few seconds later I saw a second plane coming in on a run on the same bridge, much too soon. The second plane came in very low and flat. Just as he got to the bridge, the bombs from the first plane exploded and he went right through the explosions. The plane was obscured from vision for a fraction of a second. When the plane emerged it seemed to be wallowing through the air, gaining altitude as it went. Then the plane rolled over on its back and went straight into the ground, about 150 yards from the bridge, exploding on impact and burning. The fire was still burning when we left the target area at least 15 minutes later.

The crew in addition to Lieutenant Willard Johnson of aircraft # 4382 were Second Lieutenant Fred V. Cooper (navigator), Sgt. William F. Bickel (engineer/gunner), Sgt. Dan F. Atkins (gunner) and Corporal Harry J. Charbanneau. (National Archives, Records of the Army Air Forces)

Willard's death was reported in the Bemidji Sentinel on November 24, 1944.

Former BSTC Athlete Killed Over Burma

Word was received Thursday by H. J. Erickson, coach at the Bemidji State Teachers College, telling of the death of Lieutenant Willard (Bill) Johnson of Sebeka, a former athlete at BSTC. He had been active at the local college in football, basketball, and track. Before coming to Bemidji he had starred in athletics in the Sebeka high school. Lt. Johnson was a member of the United States Air Corps and had served at Guadalcanal and other battlefronts having completed his required missions in the Southwest Pacific and had been at his home on leave last March. At that time he visited Bemidjians at the state basketball tournament in Minneapolis. The message stated that Lt. Johnson had been killed in action over Burma.[64]

---

[64] Uncredited, "Former BSTC Athlete Killed Over Burma," *Bemidji Sentinel*, November 24, 1944, 2.

DR. MICHAEL HERBERT

(Courtesy of the Wadena County-MN Historical Society)

* * * * *

The above picture, taken before the all-college dance which ended the Beaver Week activities at BSTC, shows the royal party that reigned over the student body during the week preceding the homecoming game with Eau Claire, Wisconsin. Members of the royalty were Pauline Alich of Border; Eva Mae Cann of Blackduck; Her Majesty, Queen of the Beavers, Marjorie Spilde of Halma; Ardelle Lee of Fosston; Barbara Hartness of Bemidji and Fern Englund of Bemidji.

The Northern Student
Friday, October 20th, 1944
(Bemidji State University Archives)

As the winter holidays were approaching, the students of BSTC were busy sending cards and presents to the BSTC servicemen. By the end of November of 1944, over 300 Christmas cards had been sent overseas. The cards were reprints of photographs of campus scenes. The members of the Alpha Phi Sigma sorority sent over fifteen packages of Christmas gifts overseas to former BSTC students and would be sending gifts to the servicemen still in the United States by the end of the month.

Shown in the picture are members of the Alpha Phi Sigma as they locate on the globe the whereabouts of former members in the armed forces to whom the club sent Christmas gifts. The club sent over 15 packages to servicemen stationed overseas and will also send gifts to the GI Joes still in the United States come Christmastime. The club has also purchased three $25 war bonds. The members pictured from left to right are (in the first row) Jean Currie, Daphne Chisholm, Marjorie Schofield, Eva Mae Cann, Ruth Austin and Mona Spangler; (and in the second row) Faith Fleenor, Doris Sandberg (fairly hidden in shadows), Marguerite Charlton, Miss Ruth Brune, faculty adviser, Eleanor Anderson, Don Clark, Audrey Peterson, Frances Whalen, Margaret Anderson and Frances Torgerson.

The Northern Student
Wednesday, November 22, 1944, p. 1
(Bemidji State University Archives)

The major Christmas party, sponsored by the freshman and sophomore classes, was scheduled for December 16 and included dancing, singing and a number of Christmas songs to be sung by the chorus, under the direction of Carl Thompson. The woman's chorus planned their eighth candlelight service at the First Lutheran Church. This year's concert is "Carols of the Nations."

BSTC was moving forward with the program which would allow credit for courses by returning servicemen. "The guiding principle of the program," stated Dr. C. V. Hobson, "is to give credit for what the returning veteran knows, regardless of where or how he learned it."[65] The program would allow returning servicemen up to twelve credits in related subject fields; secondly, credit would be given for subjects studied in the various army programs throughout other colleges and universities; thirdly, through experience, veterans who feel they have mastered some subject can apply for credit by showing they have taken Armed Forces Institute tests or teacher-constructed tests that show the mastery of the subject matter.

The Beaver football team played its second wartime football program and while challenged with player shortages, had an undefeated season, scoring 78 season points against the opponents 20 points.

---

[65] C. V. Hobson, "Credits for Returning Veterans," *The Northern Student*, November 22, 1944, 1.

1945

THE EIGHTH-GRADE LAB STUDENT BOND and stamp sales this academic year will be a Jeep campaign. The eighth graders are hoping to sell enough bonds and stamps to be able to purchase a Jeep, which costs about a thousand dollars. A poster of a Jeep and its parts, along with the prices of each, was hung in the junior high school hall. As the money is raised for each part, that part is covered up, showing what is left to buy. As an incentive, three films made by the Treasury Department, which were taken since the fall of France, will be shown at the regular assembly of the laboratory school.

(https://www.flickr.com/photos/lee-ekstrom/8113161226)

Robert Henry Frazer
Died in Service January 4, 1945

Robert Henry Frazer was born on May 19, 1920, in Mahnomen, Minnesota. Robert became a student at the Bemidji State Teachers College the fall quarter of 1938 and graduated the spring of 1940. During the time Robert was a student at BSTC he resided at 900 Minnesota Avenue, Bemidji. After graduating from BSTC, Robert went on to be a student at the University of Minnesota. While a student at the U of M, Robert registered for the draft on July 1, 1941, and shortly thereafter joined the Naval Reserves. Robert qualified for pilot training as he had already passed the Civilian Pilot Training course in Bemidji. Robert's training progress was reported thusly in the *Bemidji Daily Pioneer*: "Mr. and Mrs. H. S. Frazer have received word that their son, Robert H. Frazer, completes his course at Corpus Christi, Friday and will be commissioned as Ensign in the naval flying forces. He is now to take advanced training at Miami, Florida, before being assigned to duty."[66]

Frazer started his flight training in the local CPT course and went from there to Hibbing. Robert volunteered for flight training in October of 1941 at started his military flight training at the US Naval reserve aviation base in Minneapolis and upon completion was transferred to Corpus Christi, Texas, for intermediate and advanced training at this "University of the Air," the largest naval aviation training facility in the United States. Robert's training included a thorough ground training course, navigation, radio code, gunnery, bombing theory, and communications.

---

[66] Uncredited, *The Bemidji Daily Pioneer*, October 15, 1942, 1.

Bemidji Daily Pioneer. October 17, 1942, p. 2.

While in service, Lt. Frazer wrote to President Sattgast and had this to say,

> In a recent letter from Flight Lieutenant James Frazer, President Sattgast was thanked very much for arranging a copy of the *Northern Student.* The letter states, "it is certainly a pleasure to read the doings of the various groups at the college. I must confess though those names are changing, and considerable groups are unknown to me."
>
> Remember the movie "Target for Tonight" that we saw a few weeks ago? Listen to Lieut. Frazer's very interesting account concerning it:
>
> "I see that in your assembly program you have had a showing of the film "Target for Tonight." You will now have a much better idea of just what I am doing and have been doing from that picture. It is our job to train the men who operate the bombers such as you saw. In particular, if you think the work done by the Scotch navigator and the bomb aimer, you will have a fair idea of what I do, teach, and organize.

Incidentally, I had dinner with the Scotch navigator in the picture. He was sent to Canada after 30 operational trips over Germany for a refresher course. He later married a Toronto girl and took her back to England with him."[67]

On Saturday, January 22, 1944, Robert married Marie Ariette McVeety in Seattle, Washington. The newlyweds then moved to San Diego, where Robert was stationed.

On February 16, 1945, *The Bemidji Daily Pioneer* reported the Mr. and Mrs. Frazer had received a letter from the War Department that their son, Robert, was missing in action in the South Pacific Area. His parents had received previous letters telling them of Robert's participation in the Leyte Gulf campaign. Robert had last visited Bemidji in 1943 when he had a thirty-day leave.[68]

Robert was assigned to the aircraft carrier *Ommaney Bay* (CVE-79) prior to his being reported missing in action.

Ommaney Bay CVE-79. (Naval History and Heritage Command)

[67] James Frazer, *The Northern Student*, October 27, 1942, 2
[68] Uncredited, *The Bemidji Daily Pioneer*, February 16, 1945, 4.

This account of what happened to the *Ommaney Bay* on January 4, 1945, directly coincides with the reported date on Robert as being listed as missing in action.

> *Ommaney Bay* left on New Year's Day 1945 and transitted [*sic*] the Surigao Straight [*sic*] 2 days later. The next afternoon, while in the Sulu Sea, a twin-engine Japanese suicide plane penetrated the screen undetected and made for *Ommaney Bay.* The plane nicked her island then crashed her starboard side. Two bombs were released; one of them penetrated the flight deck and detonated below, setting off a series of explosions among the fully-gassed planes on the forward third of the hanger deck. The second bomb passed through the hanger deck, ruptured the fire main on the second deck, and exploded near the starboard side.
>
> Water pressure forward was lost immediately, along with power and bridge communications. Men struggling with the terrific blazes on the hangar deck soon had to abandon it because of the heavy black smoke from the burning planes and ricocheting .50 caliber ammunition. Escorts could not lend their power to the fight because of the exploding ammunition and intense heat from the fires. By 1750 (5:50 p.m.) the entire topside area had become untenable, and the stored torpedo warheads threatened to go off at any time. The order to abandon ship was given.
>
> At 1945 (7:45 p.m.) the veteran ship was sunk by a torpedo from the destroyer *Burns* (DD-588). A total of 95 Navymen were lost, including 2 killed on an assisting destroyer when

torpedo warheads on the carrier-s hangar deck finally went off.[69]

Ommaney Bay (CVE-79) burning in the Sulu Sea, off Mindanao on 4 January 1945 during the Lingayen Operation. She had been hit by a kamikaze. A destroyer is standing by with fire hoses ready. Copyright owner: Naval History and Heritage Command. Catalog#: NH 89350

Records show that Robert's body was recovered[70] and according to the National Archives, Robert is listed as being interred overseas. Robert is memorialized at the monument located at Fort William McKinley, Manila, Philippines. Robert was awarded Purple Heart and Distinguished Flying Cross posthumously.

[69] "*Ommaney Bay* (CVE-79)," Naval History and Heritage Command, accessed July 28, 2021, https://www.history.navy.mil/research/histories/ship-histories/danfs/o/ommaney_bay.html.

[70] "*USS Ommaney Bay (CVE-79)*," WreckSite, accessed July 28, 2021, https://www.wrecksite.eu/wreck.aspx?59770.

American Battle Monuments Commission

* * * * *

It was not at all unusual for servicemen on leave to stop by the college to visit classmates and faculty members. The photo below shows four ex-servicemen who stopped by the BSTC in January of 1945.

BSTC's four ex-service men are pictured in the new Beaver Union with Ensign Robert Peterson, who is back visiting the college. They are, left to right, Everett White, ex-army; Peck Brown, ex-navy; Millard Forsythe, ex-navy and Henry Rantanen, ex-army. In the background can be seen other students enjoying the ever-popular union. Most popular diversions of the collegians are whist, dancing, coke and coffee drinking and bull-sessions. For the four ex-service men it's "Battleship," a time-consuming, nerve-wracking game, which usually results in a violent argument.

The Northern Student, January 31, 1945, p. 1.
(Bemidji State University Archives)

On January 31, 1945, the eighth-grade lab school students successfully ended their Jeep purchase campaign. Over one thousand dollars in stamps and bonds were sold by the eighth-grade students to purchase the jeep. The eighth graders received a letter from the war finance committee stating, "We are very pleased to hear that you have completed the campaign to purchase a jeep. This is indeed a splendid achievement."[71] The letter contained a decal which was awarded to the students by the Treasury Department, a duplicate of the decal was placed in Washington, DC.

Courses offered in 1945 may seem odd in today's view of what higher education should consist of. One example was the Marksmanship course held.

1945 Bemidji State College Marksmanship Course.
(Bemidji State University Archives)

The college continued to gear up for returning veterans by making sure that the returning veterans were aware of what their benefits were. The returning veterans were to be made aware that if he is disabled he is eligible for vocational rehabilitation, including

---

[71] Uncredited, *The Northern Student*, January 31, 1945, 1.

up to four years of training in the field he desires and is best suited for, secondly, under the GI Bill of Rights, any honorably discharged veteran is entitled to one year of higher education, and if his schooling was interrupted, he is eligible for as many months as his service record. So in essence, it would be one full year plus as many months as he was enlisted. Bemidji State Teachers College participated in this program and was recognized by the Veterans Administration as already participating. Bemidji State Teachers College offered ex-servicemen assistance in four additional ways; will give up to twelve quarter hours of credit in physical education given that the serviceman completed basic training; gives up to sixteen quarter hours for correspondence work carried through the Armed Forces Institute, if those courses are included in the college catalog or are similar enough to substitute for those courses; through examination to earn credit in courses where a transcript cannot be provided; and lastly, assist the veteran in applying for his rights under vocational rehabilitation or the GI Bill. The service officer of the local Legion post was given as just one resource available for returning servicemen.

February of 1945 marked the end of the basketball season, where the Beavers were titled Co-Champions, along with Mankato State Teachers College, with a winning record of ten wins and four losses. The Footlight Guild held its "Big Top carnival" on February 16, students tried to double their cardboard money at the carnival games such as the ring-toss, bingo, and weight-guessing booths. There was a sideshow which featured dancing and singing acts as well as parodies on BSTC life. Hot dogs, pink lemonade, and caramel apples were served, and the evening was concluded by an auction where the students bid on amusing items such a cabbage, cookies, candy, and pickled pigs' feet. The last, and most sought after item for sale at the auction was a pack of Luckies (cigarettes) for the amazing sum of $10,000 cardboard dollars.

There was a contest held fall quarter for the lyrics for a new college pep song, which was won by Joyce Worth, and the music was to be set by Don Stowell, who was the naval bandmaster on the USS *Hornet*. Musician First Class Stowell completed the music to the lyrics, but due to censorship, was unable to send the finished work back to BSTC. Stowell writes, "I have the music to the song finished, but we are prohibited from sending such things in the mail. I guess you will have to wait until I reach the good old U.S.A. before I can get it to you. I feel it is pretty good, but of course the thing that counts is if and all the rest like it."[72] Other notes of interest in the February 28 edition of the *Northern Student* included that the female students were taking to the stairway banisters for pleasure rides, much to the displeasure of the janitors who were responsible for cleaning the heel marks off the adjoining walls. Some of the female students were receiving perfumes from admirers who were serving in France. Altogether it's "Ooh-la-la."

Donald Richard Jones
Died in Service February 11, 1945

Donald Jones. (Photo by Jim Winsness)

Donald graduated from the Bemidji High School in 1942 and then attended the Bemidji State Teachers College in the fall of 1942.

---

[72] Donald Stowell, *The Northern Student*, February 28, 1945, 1.

Donald registered for the draft on December 22, 1942, in Bemidji. Donald entered the Army on July 9, 1943, and was assigned to Company K, 185th Infantry Regiment, Fortieth Infantry Division. After being stationed at Camp Pickett, Virginia, on October 20, 1944, Donald was sent to the South Pacific and New Britain Island. In December of 1943, the Fortieth Division was moved to Guadalcanal for further training and limited combat patrol. At that time, the Fortieth Division was made part of the First Marine Amphibious Corps. The Fortieth then moved to Cape Gloucester on New Britain Island and relieved the First Marine Division. The Fortieth then conducted combat operations until November 27, 1944. After the Fortieth Division was relieved by the Fifth Australian Division, the Fortieth gathered at Borgen Bay and left for the Philippines.

It was noted in the Saturday, December 16, 1944, evening edition of the *Bemidji Daily Pioneer* that Donald was currently stationed in the New Britain Islands. Prior to being moved to the New Britain Islands Donald was serving in New Guinea. The article mentions that Donald would like to hear from his Bemidji friends.

After stopovers on New Guinea and Manus Island, the Fortieth Division landed in the Lingayen area of Luzon at around 09:30 a.m. on January 9, 1945, and met light resistance. That was followed up with another landing at Bamban where the division faced heavy opposition from the main Japanese force.

While his company was taking a hill near Clark Field on February 11, 1945, Donald was shot in the right wrist, which ultimately led to his death. Immediately after his death, Donald was buried at Fort Stotsenburg, Philippines, following a military funeral. Later, Donald's body was moved to the national military cemetery at Manila. In 1949, Donald's remains were brought back to Minnesota where he was laid at his final resting place at the Oakdale Cemetery, Crookston, Minnesota. All of Donald's immediate family (parents and four siblings) are deceased.

The following two articles in the *Northern Student* details Donald's activities while at the BSTC as well as the circumstances of his death.

T-5 Donald Jones Killed in the Philippines

Word has been received that T/5 Donald Jones of the army infantry and former student at BSTC was killed in action on the island of Luzon in the Philippines on February 11, 1945, after having escaped injury in combat on New Guinea and New Britain Island. T/5 Jones entered college in 1942 and was drafted into the army in the summer of 1943. During this year at BSTC he was active in sports as captain of the tumbling team and member of the football team. He was also active in various music organizations on the campus. He graduated from Bemidji high school in 1942 and as a member of the band and drama club. He was to be seen in various circles of the community as a member of the Elks Band and curling team. He was also employed for a time at the box factory.[73]

* * * * *

Mr. and Mrs. R. H. Jones of Upper Darby, Pa., and formerly of Bemidji, have received a letter from Capt. M. Dahl, who tells of the death of their son, Donald. The letter states, "The officers and men of Company K wish to extend their heartfelt sympathy and understanding to you both. Our loss of a comrade in arms does not compare to your loss of a son, but has been keenly felt, and is a real blow to us all. "Cpl. Jones was killed Feb. 1, while participating in an attack on 'Hill 1000' which was strongly held

[73] Uncredited, "T-5 Donald Jones Killed in Philippines," *The Northern Student*, April 25, 1945, 2.

by the enemy. Despite intense enemy machine-gun fire, rifle, and mortar fire, he jumped to his feet when the attack order was given and took a leading part in the assault. His utter fearless conduct made him a mark for enemy fire. He died instantly, without pain or disfigurement. "It may be some consolation to know that your son died a hero's death, which every member of this company has sworn to avenge. It may also be some comfort to know that we have killed 15 of the enemy for every comrade we have lost. Cpl. Jones was buried with full military honors, Feb. 12, at ASAF Calayo cemetery."[74]

* * * * *

As winter takes its good time in leaving northern Minnesota, the students of Bemidji State Teachers College were starting to get a little stir-crazy in April. It was noted that pranks were becoming more common, and the faculty were not immune! April marked someone (the finger being pointed at a prominent BSTC professor) had put a white mouse in the faculty women's lounge. One male student poured a bottle of the "best ten-cent perfumes available" on the head of a female student, who was then avoided by all the remainder of the day.

Former president of the BSTC, Captain C. R. Sattgast, had been placed in charge of documents recording all American and British fliers who were downed in Germany. The documents are expected to reveal the fate of thousands of allied airmen listed as missing in action. The master file, which was located in Buchenbuhl, was reported to contain information on over 45,000 allied airmen. The documents report that over one million dollars in various currencies had been taken from the captive airmen. As a result of Captain

---

[74] M. Dahl, Letter to R. H. Jones, *The Northern Student*, May 4, 1945, 3.

Sattgast's investigative work on this file, the arrest of a Nazi propagandist, Dr. Frederick Aughagen, was made.

CAPTAIN C. R. SATTGAST

The Northern Student, April 1945, p. 3.
(Bemidji State University Archives)

In the "What Goes, Alumni?" weekly article the following was quoted:

> We know you'd like to share in paying tribute to
> the service of the following BSTC students, for
> whom gold stars have been added to the service
> flag: T/5 Donald Jones, Army Infantry, was killed
> in action in the Philippines on February 11th, hav-
> ing seen action in New Guinea and New Britain
> Island prior to Luzon, the place of his death… Lt.
> Roger Hilstad, AAF, is reported killed in action
> in the European theatre, having failed to return
> to his base in England following a mission over
> European enemy territory on May 12, 1944. He
> had been awarded the Air Medal and Oak Leaf

Cluster for exceptional meritorious service... former student Kenneth Gregg, Lt. AAF, after been reported missing in action, has now been declared killed in action July 21, 1944. He was pilot of a B-17. Former student Lt. Jack Sansom is a B-29 pilot stationed on Saipan-his wife Vivian Maxfield, meanwhile is pursuing her journalistic career on one of the St. Paul weeklies.[75]

Former student navy Lt. Robert E. Huffman was awarded the Bronze Star, the account stated as "when his landing craft was damaged and left burning during the invasion of Normandy he swam 150 yards to the beach which was raked by enemy artillery mortars, machineguns, and snipers. After seeing that his men were properly dug in, he boldly exposed himself to enemy fire for several hours as he moved about the beach directing operations." Lt Huffman was graduated from BSTC in 1940 with majors in art and social studies previous to his enlistment. Last fall he visited BSTC, at which time he talked to the art classes about his experiences in England and France."[76] Corporal Joe Nyquist, stationed somewhere in the Philippines, writes that "*Bob Worth*, Ed Ingersoll, and I have spent quite a bit of time talking over Bemidji." Due to the time it took mail to get from overseas, by the time this was printed in the April 25, 1945, edition of the *Northern Student*, Bob Worth had been killed in action.

Jack R. Sansom
Died in Service April 25, 1945

Jack Sansom was born on September 14, 1919, and left Bemidji State Teacher's College to report for duty at Fort Snelling, Minnesota, on July 8, 1940, being listed as 5'8" tall and weighing 133 pounds. When Jack was in Bemidji, he lived at 321 Ninth Street, which was rented by Jack's uncle, W. S. Dahlgren, for $18 a month (1940 dol-

---

[75] Uncredited, "What Goes Alumni?" *The Norther Student*, April 25, 1945, 3.
[76] Uncredited, *The Northern Student*, April 15, 1945, 4.

lars!). Prior to living in Bemidji, Jack resided in Wahpeton, North Dakota. By August 10, 1942, Jack had graduated as a staff sergeant from Chanute Field School of the Army Air Forces Technical Training Command. Jack was trained there in various technical operations vital to the maintenance of Army Air Force fighting aircraft.[77]

It was reported in the *Bemidji Daily Pioneer* in November of 1942 that Jack had reported to the Army Air Forces preflight school, located at Maxwell Field, Alabama, to begin the second phase of flight training. It was noted that Jack had served twenty-seven months in the Army before being appointed an air cadet and started his flight training at Chanute Field prior to reporting to Maxwell Field. Jack would spend nine weeks at Maxwell Field for the second phase of training. Jack began training as a member of the 499th Heavy Bombing Group at Davis-Monthan Air Base in Tucson, Arizona (The 499th Bomb Group of the Seventy-Third Bomb wing was activated on November 20, 1943.), and then the group transferred to Salina, Kansas. The group first started training in the B-17 "Flying Fortress" as the new B-29 "Superfortress" was still in short supply. in the new B-29 Superfortress at the Davis-Monthan Air Base in Tucson, Arizona on April 8, 1944, and then transferred to Salina, Kansas, for training on April 8, 1944. The Bomb Group consisted of four squadrons—the 877th, 878th, 879th, and 880th—Jack being assigned to the 877th squadron. As was noted in the *Unofficial History of the 499th Group* by author Prentiss "Mick" Burkett,

> In May of 1943 the squadron began receiving a newer aircraft, the B-29 Superfortress, which most aircrews felt was a vast improvement over the B-17s which they had started their combat training with. The majority of their combat training was completed by October of 1944.
>
> Their new destination would be the newly fought over and acquired pacific island of Saipan. The ground crews left for Saipan in July of 1944,

---

[77] Uncredited, *The Bemidji Daily Pioneer*, August 10, 1942, 4.

while ten aircrews were selected to fly their aircraft to Isely Field, Saipan and the other ten aircrews took trains to Hamilton Airfield in northern California and then transported by the Air Transport Command, with most of the aircrews arriving in Saipan by late November.

Isely Field, Saipan 1945. By United States Army Air Forces—(http://atheyfamily.org/B29/73rdBombWing. htm XXI Bomber Command Photos, US National Archives, College Park MD Campus, Public Domain.)

Life on Saipan was taxing, as the sweltering weather accompanied by frequent heavy rains, and primarily night enemy air raids on the field made for a less that comfortable experience. Gradually conditions improved with the move from living in tents to Quonset huts, paved roads, chapels, theaters and clubs which all made life more bearable. Most importantly, the enemy air raids ceased after the Japanese lost the island of Iwo Jima to allied forces and thus unable to use the airfield as a staging base.[78]

The first group combat mission was held on November 24, 1944, the target being Tokyo, which was the very first strike by B-29s on the Japanese main island. Fortunately, while some Japanese fighter resistance was encountered, none of the group's bombers were shot down. Coincidently, while the group was on their mission, their base came under enemy attack, which caused damage to the base facilities as well as one Superfortress.

The bomber group lost its first Superfortress on a mission held on December 13, 1944. The group was on a mission to Mitsubishi aircraft plant, which was located Nagoya, Japan. The crew captained by Lieutenant Ledbetter was hit by antiaircraft flack over the target area and still managed to make it back to Saipan but had to crash land in Magicienne bay upon which time all of the crew were lost.

On April 24, 1945, Lieutenant Jack Sansom was part of the crew of the V Square 11, B-29 Superfortress led by Lieutenant Ray Antonucci on a mission over Japan.

The Lt. Ray Antonucci Crew. (The Unofficial History of the 499th Group)

---

[78] Prentiss Burkett, *The Unofficial History of the 499th Group.* (Temple City, California: Historical Aviation Album, 1981), 65. Uncredited. *The Bemidji Daily Pioneer*, February 16, 1945.

According to official US Army reports, Sansom's aircraft successfully conducted its bombing run and was continuing on to a secondary target when the aircraft was struck by enemy aircraft gunfire. Shortly after being hit by the enemy aircraft gunfire, other aircraft in the group reported seeing smoke coming from the cockpit and right wing of the aircraft. Shortly thereafter, other group aircraft reported seeing ten parachutes dropping from the burning aircraft. The V Square 11 had a crew of eleven that day. Another B-29 from the formation dropped a life raft in the area where they parachutists were guessed to have landed in the water. According to the brother of one of the crewmen, Sergeant Angelo Dindo, Louis Dindo, reported that Sergeant Jack Kropf was the only crewman who had reportedly survived the war. According the Dindo's account, Kropf reported that he was the last crewman to bail out of the aircraft and landed alone in the water. Kropf located the life raft that had been dropped by the other B-29 in the group and was shortly thereafter found by the Japanese Navy and spent the remainder of the war as a prisoner of war. According to the brother of Sergeant Angelo Dindo, Louis Dindo, Sergeant Jack Kropf (V Square 11's tail gunner) was the only crew member who survived the war. Sergeant Kropf was freed from a Japanese prisoner of war camp at the end of the war.

The pilot of the B-29, Square V 11, Lieutenant Ray Antonucci, was found by a Japanese fisherman two miles off the shore of Japan and buried in Japan. At the conclusion of the war, the fisherman who had found Antonucci was honorable enough to show the allied occupation army of General Douglas McArthur where Antonucci had been buried. Lieutenant Antonucci was then identified by the laundry markings on his uniform.

There was no information on the remainder of the crew of Square V 11 after the aircraft went into the Sea of Japan, so the final fate of Lieutenant Jack Sansom remains a mystery.

Jack was posthumously awarded the Air Medal and the Purple Heart. Jack Samson's burial site is located the Fairview Memorial Gardens, Wahpeton, Richland County, North Dakota. Jack Samson is also memorialized at the Honolulu memorial in Hawaii (see below).

Cenotaph: National Memorial Cemetery of
the Pacific. Honolulu, Hawaii.

Carrington Cemetery. Carrington, North
Dakota. (Photo by Brent Bruderer)

Amel Hocking
Died in Service May 24, 1945

While the war in Europe ended in May of 1945, the fighting still continued in the Pacific theater with the war with Japan. Amel T. Hocking was born in 1920, the son of Garfield and Margaret Hocking, in Hibbing, Minnesota. Amel Hocking, as a student at Bemidji State Teachers College, was a member of the Beaver football squad as well as being involved in other extracurricular activities. The 340th Engineer Construction Battalion left the California aboard the transport Tennant on March 5, 1944. The ship docked for the first time since leaving California at Townsville, Australia, and were immediately moved to the Royal Army Air Force (RAAF) base at Darwin to begin construction of aircraft hangers, taxiways, and facilities for the B-29 Superfortress bombers soon to be arriving. On August 17, 1944, the battalion left Darwin aboard two liberty ships, the *Don Marquis* and the *Sylvestre Escalante*. They soon arrived Hollandia, Dutch New Guinea. The men then moved inland and established camp.

The short time the men were in Hollandia, they were prepared for their participation in Operation Interlude, the invasion of Morotai (one of Indonesia's most northern islands). On September 4, 1944, 300 men of the battalion left Hollandia on an LST (Landing Ship Troop) and arrived at Morotai, Netherlands East Indies on D-Day, September 15, 1944. By September 25, the remainder of the battalion had arrived and were put to work building roads, piers, and buildings.

On January 9, 1945, the battalion was moved from Morotai to the Island of Luzon. The battalion spent ten months on Luzon building roads, bridges, buildings, and mine and booby trap removal. During this entire time, the men were under contact danger of being attacked by the remaining Japanese forces. On May 24, 1945, Amel, along with Technician Fifth Gerald C. Smith and Technician Fifth Julius Zupan were killed when an enemy mine was detonated.

KILLED IN ACTION

While helping in the push toward Baguio, three members of the unit lost their lives when an enemy mine was set off. They were doing what is expected of every soldier, namely: their duty. But more than that, they gave their lives.

Funeral services were held for Corporal Amel T. Hockings, Technician 5th, Gerald C. Schmidt and Technician 5th, Julius Zupan; all of Company C. These men were laid to rest at Santa Barbara Cemetery, in Pangasinan Province, Luzon.

340th Engineers in the Pacific, United States
Army, Engineer Battalion, 340th. 1946.

Three men were initially interred at the Santa Barbara Cemetery, Pangasinan Province, Luzon. Amel's grave was later moved to the Manila American Cemetery and Memorial, Old Lawton Avenue, Taguig, Metro Manila, Philippines. After the Japanese surrender, the men of the battalion waited anxiously the return to the United States, and by November of 1945, the majority of the men had been shipped home. By the end of December 1945, the battalion was inactivated. The family of Amel reported to the *Bemidji Daily Pioneer* his death in June of 1945, being killed in action at Luzon, Philippines, the largest island in the chain.

From these honored dead we take increased devotion to that cause for which they gave the last full measure of devotion :
Abraham Lincoln

JAMIE H. ALEXANDER
ALMON J. CHELSSON
RONNIE CURRAN
JOE B. GONZALES
EUGENE E. HALL
AMEL T. HOCKING
JOSEPH M. KOTZ
THOMAS W. PRICE
GERALD C. SCHMIDT
GARLAND W. STEELE
WILLIAM E. STEPHENSEN
JULIUS ZUPAN

340th Engineers in the Pacific, United States
Army, Engineer Battalion, 340th, 1946.

* * * * *

The surrender of Nazi Germany in May of 1945 was welcome news by everyone at the Bemidji State Teachers College. While the war against Japan was still ongoing, end of academic year activities took place as usual. Monday, May 24, marked the day for the annual senior picnic, which was held at Rocky Point. It was reported that the food was plentiful and very good. The only distractions came from the mosquitoes and the occasional discovery of a wood tick. On

Sunday, June 3, an afternoon tea was hosted by President and Mrs. A. C. Clark, which was followed by baccalaureate services which took place that evening at the First Lutheran Church. There were twenty-one four-year graduates and twenty-four two-year graduates that year. On the following Wednesday, there was a garden party held for the graduates in front of Deputy Hall, given by the faculty and alumni. The student paper noted the return of veterans to campus.

Robert Worth
Died in Service April 16, 1945

Robert was born in Bemidji, Minnesota, in 1923. Robert graduated from the Bemidji High School in 1941, where he was a captain of the football team as well as a member of the basketball team and the high school band. Immediately after high school, Robert worked for Van Roy Miller in Kansas City, Kansas, until November of 1942. During that time in Kansas City, Robert registered for the draft on June 30, 1942. Robert left Kansas City and returned to Bemidji, where he then enrolled as a student at the Bemidji State Teachers College. Robert attended BSTC until February 25, 1943, when he entered military service.

Robert entered his service with the army, and it was noted in the *Northern Student* on June 8, 1943, that he (Private Worth) could be reached at Company G of the 114th Regiment, APO 44, Fort Lewis, Washington. Robert was also listed in that same edition of the paper on the Honor Roll of Our Servicemen.

In August of that year, Robert's parents, Mr. and Mrs. Albert Worth, received word from now Sergeant Worth, that he had arrived safely somewhere in the South Pacific. Robert was sent overseas in July of 1944 and was with the first invasion troops to land on Leyte in October of 1944.

On April 24, 1945, Robert's parents (who then resided at 518 Beltrami Avenue, Bemidji, Minnesota) had been notified via V-mail from Robert, now first sergeant with the Ninety-Sixth Infantry Division, that he had been in combat action in the central region of Okinawa. During that fighting, he had been wounded by Japanese artillery the first part of April. Robert wrote he had one abdominal operation at the base and was being evacuated to Guam, Hawaii, or some other hospital where he expected to have another operation before he could recover entirely. He wrote that he hoped it would be Hawaii where he could get some ice cream and milk.

Friday morning, May 18, 1945, Mr. and Mrs. Worth received notice that their son, Robert was dead. With the medical treatment he received in Okinawa, Robert was unable to recover well enough to be transported to a more advanced medical facility. Robert is buried at the Fort Snelling National Cemetery, Minneapolis, Minnesota.

(Photograph by Steve Edquist)

* * * * *

Former student T/Sgt. Bill Conner writes,

> These are truly busy days for all of us here in Austria. These people should be treated sternly for

this reason: almost without exception, the man on the street was for Hitler's policies as long as they were succeeding. By 1939 almost everyone was for him. He had taken the Rhineland, achieved reunion with Austria, restored the international prestige of the Fatherland, had rebuilt Germany's military, and put bread in every mouth, even though they had guns instead of butter. They supported him because he gave them material wealth, a sense of superiority and a promise of military glory which plays a great role in German thinking. Only when the Russian scheme fell through and the losses in men began to mount without new material gains did the opposition now culminate in these last-minute "Freedom Movements," which are actually betrayals of all a people who have presumably been fighting for six long years. We welcome them, yet, because they save American lives; but we don't trust them because they came too late.[79]

Those BSTC former students serving in the Pacific theater were glad to hear of the war in Europe being over but realized they were still at war. This is exemplified by some of the responses to the news by those serving in the Philippines. Former student Lt. Laverne Nies describes some of the reactions by soldiers of the war in Europe ending:

Two of the guys playing cards said, "So what?" The third was more typical of our reception of the news—"Who's deal?" So much for the news.[80]

---

[79] Bill Conner, Letter to *The Northern Student*, *The Northern Student*, June 6, 1945, 3.
[80] Laverne Nies, Letter to *The Northern Student*, *The Northern Student*, June 6, 1945, 3.

The Northern Student marked yet another wartime death of a former student,

> A recent message from the War Department announced the death of Sgt. Bob Worth. He was killed on Okinawa, where he was with the 96th Infantry Division. On behalf of the faculty and student body of BSTC, the Norther Student staff members wish to express their sympathy to the family of the deceased.[81]

The fall of 1945 started yet another academic year and it was quite noticeable the influx of veterans enrolling at BSTC. The fall of 1945 noted an enrollment increase overall of 20 percent with fifty-five men registered.

Nine of BSTC veterans are shown in the above picture relaxing on the campus. They are, (back row) left to right: Evie White, Bob Johnson, Peck Brown, Gene Campbell, Hank Rantanen, and Chuck Haugen. (Front row) Allen Westerlund, Francis Bussey, and Art Nord. Not shown are Mike Forsythe, Harry Stoner, Jack Sugrue, Ray Razee, Tex Brannan, and Wally Wakelum.

The Northern Student, Wednesday, October 24, 1945. (Bemidji State University Archives)

---

[81] Uncredited, *The Northern Student*, June 6, 1945, 3.

Bruce Johnson
Died in Service August 1, 1945

Bruce was from Boy River (Cass County) Minnesota and graduated from high school in the spring of 1941. Bruce started at the
Bemidji State Teachers College that same fall. On June 30, 1942,
Bruce registered for the draft in Walker, Minnesota. Bruce was listed
as being 5'7" tall weighing 135 pounds.

United States Veterans Affairs Archives

In the June 8, 1943, supplement of the Northern Student Bruce
was listed as S2C (seaman second class) Bruce Johnson, Co. 46-43
OGU, United States Naval Training Station, Farragut, Idaho.

Bruce was eventually sent overseas, and at the time of his death,
he was listed as a crew member on a flight in the Hawaii area. Bruce's
classification upon death on the WWII Navy, Marine Corps and
Coast Guard Casualty List, was listed as "combat," upon the recov-
ery of Bruce's body, which was interred in a common gave along with
AMM3 (aviation machinists mate) Joseph D. Irons at the Oahu-
Schofield Barracks Mausoleum, Hawaii.

Military archival records show that, interestingly, you will note that Bruce's tombstone also includes the name of Joseph D. Irons. The records show that on December 9, 1949, Bruce was interred from a common grave which included Joseph Irons. Bruce had previously had his remains located at the Schofield Barracks Mausoleum, number 2, Hawaiian Islands. Both Bruce and Joseph had their remains brought back to the United States in May of 1949 and were buried together at the Zachary Taylor National Cemetery, Louisville, Kentucky.

(United States Veterans Affairs Office Archives)

The Wars End

While World War II officially ended September 2, 1945, with the surrender of the Japanese, I feel it appropriate that I note the passing of two other former students of the Bemidji State Teachers College who went into military service during the war, but died shortly after the war, either due to war-related injury or still serving in the military. These two former students were Wilber (Will) Erickson and Charles Marmorine.

Will Erickson, of Red Lake, Minnesota, attended Bemidji High School and immediately thereafter entered the Bemidji State Teachers College. Will served as the editor for the *Northern Student* while a student at the college and the year that the paper was awarded the All-American award from the Columbia Press Association. Will entered the army in the spring of 1941 and was aboard the USS *Coolidge* when it eventually sank. The USS *Coolidge* was transporting troops to the base at Espiritu Santo on October 26, 1942. As it approached the island, using the largest harbor available, the ship struck an underwater mine. The ship's captain, realizing that the ship would sink, attempted to run the ship aground. The ship, however, got caught on a coral reef prior to reaching the beach, and in ninety minutes, 5,390 men were able to get safely ashore. There were two fatal casualties listed. The ship, shortly thereafter, slid into the harbor, and now sits submerged in seventy feet of water.

The USS *Coolidge* being abandoned after striking a mine.
(United States Army in World War—The War Department—
Global Logistics and Strategy 1940–1943, p. 394)

Will attained the rank of staff sergeant and was later wounded on Guadalcanal, being one of the few who survived in his company. Will also participated in the Solomon Islands campaign where he served as an advance scout for the field artillery. Will was then hospitalized in New Zealand and later transferred to Modesto, California, then to Fort Snelling, Minnesota, where he served as a military police officer on trains that ran between Minneapolis and Kansas City. Still suffering from injuries and illnesses he received while in the Pacific (malaria and amnesia), Will was treated at the US Army hospital located at Camp Carlson, Colorado.

From Camp Carlson, Will received his honorable discharge and returned home to Red Lake on September 6. Will was awarded four Bronze Stars and a Purple Heart. Will was pictured on large posters during the Sixth War Loan in 1943, showing the wounded being evacuated from the Pacific.

Produced by the United States Treasury Department

Just eleven days after Will returned from military service, September 17, at 9:00 p.m., he was involved in an accident by the Bemidji Country Club where his vehicle rolled over. Will lost consciousness and was transported to the local hospital where he never regained consciousness. Will was alone at the time of the accident, and the accident was attributed to his sudden attacks related to his malaria and amnesia, causing him to lose control of his vehicle.

Will is buried in the Greenwood Cemetery in Bemidji, Minnesota.

Charles Marmorine began his college experience at BSTC in the fall of 1941. Charles was one of the students that entered the BSTC as a high school valedictorian of the Gonvick high school. Charles enlisted in the Army reserves on October 15, 1942. Charles was active in college activities and was noted as being in the A Cappella choir; LSA; church choir, and associate editor of the Northern Student.

February 20, 1943, Charles, a member of the Army Air Corps Reserve, was called up to active duty. Charles left for training in Waco, Texas, and then receiving transport flight training at Austin,

Texas. Charles was able to return on leave in April of 1944 and on Sunday, April 24, married Miss Garnette Nichols. By then, Charles was a second lieutenant and had earned his pilot's wings.

Charles was assigned transport duties in the C-47 "Goonie Bird" from a base approximately fifteen miles from Shanghai, China. While assigned there, he was promoted to First Lieutenant and had been rewarded the Distinguished Flying Cross and Air Medal. Charles had been flying from that region for just over a year.

Charles and his aircraft were reported missing on September 27, 1945. In November of 1945, the military reported that Charles had died in an aircraft accident.

It would be remiss to not acknowledge the faculty who either were drafted or enlisted in World War II. Some of the faculty shown below did return to Bemidji State Teachers College after the war was over and some moved on to other institutions of higher learning.

The Bemidji Daily Pioneer, Special Edition, January 4, 1960.

The Northern Student, Wednesday, October 24, 1945. (Bemidji State University Archives)

This was the last notice of the passing of former students who served and died in military service during World War II in the student paper. Sadly, this did not mark the end of former students' deaths while serving in the military shortly after the formal end of hostilities. Lt. *Charles Marmorine* was reported missing in action in China since September 27 of 1945 and was declared killed in an airplane accident. Word had also been received that Lt. *Gilbert Lizer*, another former student, had previously been reported missing in action had been killed October 2 in the Okinawa vicinity while serving on a seaplane tender.

After Four Years, World Is at Peace on Thanksgiving Day; Let Us Make This Permanent

The fires of death and destruction which have ravaged the world for the past four years have been snuffed out. Germany and Japan have surrendered. For the first time in four long, exhausting years, the world is again at peace on Thanksgiving day. On this Thanksgiving day we can be thankful that our homeland was not invaded, that our people have not gone unfed, that our homes and cities have not been destroyed, that many of our men have returned to take up life where they left it—in short we can be thankful that the horrors of war are over and that peace and harmony will soon be ours.

But while we are thanking God for these things let us not be indifferent to the great mass of people who may share in the ritual of the holiday, but for whom the spirit of Thanksgiving is stifled because they are still dazed by the catastrophe of war.

The coming year will certainly show great progress in the direction of peace. But let us remember that peace is not won overnight. While we are thanking God that this war is over, let us pray that we may not give way to unthinking hatred toward nations whose policies we may question or cannot understand, an attitude which sows the seeds of mistrust and suspicion . . . that we may have the understanding necessary to deal with the racial problem which confronts us both here and abroad and take definite steps to solve it . . . that we may have the knowledge and insight necessary to turn the atomic bomb from a weapon of destruction into an instrument of peace . . . and that we may have the wisdom and patience for it will take many years necessary to prevent another war and bring lasting peace to the people of all nations.

The Northern Student, November 21, 1945, p. 2.
(Bemidji State University Archives)

During halftime at a home football game on October of 1945, there was an "impressive" memorial service held in honor of all those who had served in the military in WWII, especially those who had died in service. There was a flag ceremony as well as a short talk by Reverend Boyle. The local state Guard unit comprised the firing squad, which remembered the over 500 citizens Bemidji and Beltrami County who served in the military. A quartet sang "Abide with Me" while all of the stadium lights were turned off, except one, which was aimed at the American flag at the east end of the football field. There were a number of Gold Star mothers present who were given rose corsages. The Gold Star mothers who were present were Mrs. Harry Roese, Mrs. Joe Shirk, Mrs. H. M. Cords, Mrs. Roy Gregg, Mrs.

John McCormick, Mrs. Albert Worth, Mrs. Frank Getchell, Mrs. O. E. Erickson, and Mrs. Olaf Johnson. The memorial service was concluded with all in attendance singing "America."

In the years following the end of the second world war, enrollments by returning veterans increased the student population. Life for college students was slowly returning to what one could consider "normal" by way of Homecoming celebrations, the routine of attending classes, college hijinks, and other events that make up the college experience would no longer be shadowed by the tragedy of the deaths of their fellow students. Sadly, the deaths of their fellow students would forever mar their college experience and shape their lives forever more.

NOTES

1941

1 Pettus, Randall H., ed. *Who's Who. The Official Who's Who Among Students in American Universities and Colleges. Volume VIII. 1941–1942.* Tuscaloosa, Alabama: Randall Publishing Company. 1942.

2 Uncredited. *The Northern Student*, December 2, 1939.

1942

3 Arnold, Edgar. *The Northern Student.* Vol. XV. February 1942.

4 Anonymous. *The Northern Student.* Vol. XV. February 1942.

5 Rankow, Roland. "Personal Interview with Dennis Hill." Camp 59 Survivors. Last modified June 9, 2013. https://camp59survivors.com/2013/06/09/roland-rakows-story-an-update/.

6 Johnson, Steven P. "Roland Rankow's Story—An Update—Interview." US Defense POW/Missing Personnel Office. November 27, 2011. https://camp59survivors.com/2013/06/09/roland-rakows-story-an-update/.

7 Uncredited. "College Approved for Pre-Officer Training." *The Bemidji Daily Pioneer*, August 29, 1942.

8 Perry, Helen. "So You're Wondering What BSTC Will Be Like This Year." *The Northern Student*, September 29, 1942.

9 Uncredited. "Homecoming Week." *The Bemidji Daily Pioneer*, October 2, 1942.

10 Uncredited. "What Do You Want for Christmas?" *Northern Student,* December 16, 1942.

11 Uncredited. "Alumni and Former Students Serving in the Military to Receive the Northern Student." *The Northern Student*, Volume XVI No. 5 (December 16, 1942), 1.

[12] Johnson, Elaine. "Conservation Committee Organized." *The Northern Student* Volume XVI, December 16, 1942.

1943

[13] Uncredited. "Rites for James Koefod at Rockford Sunday." *The Bemidji Daily Pioneer*, January 20, 1943.

[14] Uncredited. *All Hands Naval Bulletin*. Bureau of Naval Personnel (July 1943), 61.

[15] Buell, Harold. *Dauntless Helldivers*. New York: Crown Publishing, 1991.

[16] Uncredited. *The Bemidji Daily Pioneer*, January 30, 1943.

[17] Uncredited. *The Bemidji Daily Pioneer*, February 11, 1943.

[18] Uncredited. *The Northern Student*, February 17, 1943.

[19] McCormick, Jack. "Jack McCormick Tells of Life in England." *Bemidji Sentinel*, January 1, 1942.

[20] Uncredited. *The Bemidji Daily Pioneer*. January 30, 1943.

[21] Uncredited. *Thus Writes the Warrior. The Bemidji Daily Pioneer*, February 9, 1943.

[1] Hoganson, Mona. *Just Comment. The Northern Student*, February 24, 1943.

[22] Adams, F. R. "Teacher Shortage." *The Northern Student*, February 24, 1943.

[23] Uncredited. "In Memorandum." *The Northern Student*, February 24, 1943.

[24] Hoganson, Mona. *Just Comment. The Northern Student*, April 13, 1943.

[25] Uncredited. "Our Men in Service." *The Bemidji Daily Pioneer*, July 21, 1942.

[26] Uncredited. "Two Local Men Missing in Action." *The Bemidji Daily Pioneer*, May 29, 1943.

[27] Woods, Wiley. *Legacy of the 90th Bombardment Group "The Jolly Rogers."* Paducah, Kentucky: Turner Publishing Company, 1994.

[28] *Ibid.*

[29] Pickett, Russell S. "WWII Memorial Pages." RussPickett. http://russ-pickett.com/.

[30] Daggy, R. H. "Daggy Writes from South Pacific Area." *The Northern Student*, June 8, 1943.

[31] Roese, Harry. *Thus Writes the Warrior. The Northern Student*, June 8, 1943.

[32] United States Army Air Corps. Missing Air Crew Report (MACR). Filed August 25, 1943.

[33] Clark, A. C. "Dr. Sattgast Given Leave of Absence, Dr. Clark Appointed College President." *The Bemidji Daily Pioneer*, August 24, 1943.

[34] McNutt, Paul V. *The Northern Student*, September 29, 1943.

[35] Uncredited, "For Him and Others Like Him." *The Northern Student*, October 27, 1943.

[36] Uncredited. *The Northern Student*, November 24, 1943.

[37] *Ibid.*

[38] Uncredited. "Reasons to be Thankful." *The Northern Student*, November 24, 1943.

[39] Daggy, Richard. "Lieut. Daggy Speaks at College Tonight." *The Bemidji Daily Pioneer*, December 14, 1943.

[40] Uncredited. *The Northern Student*, December 15, 1943.

1944

[41] Coder, Kenneth. *The Northern Student*, February 23, 1944.

[42] Uncredited. "Get in Line Girls… There's a Man Loose Again." *The Northern Student*, February 23, 1944.

[43] Shock, John. *The Northern Student*, February 23, 1944.

[44] Cords, Howard. *The Bemidji Daily Pioneer*, February 10,1943.

[45] Uncredited. *The Northern Student*, April 26, 1944.

[46] Hakkerup, Bob. *The Northern Student*, April 26, 1944.

[47] Uncredited. *The Bemidji Daily Pioneer*, May 29, 1944.

[48] Uncredited. "Lieut. Roger Hilstad Is Reported Killed." *The Bemidji Daily Pioneer*, March 13, 1945.

[49] Van Eyck, Manuel F. *Silent Heroes*. Paducah, Kentucky: Turner Publishing, 2002.

[50] Uncredited. *The Bemidji Daily Pioneer*, August 31, 1942.

[51] Uncredited. "Lieut. Lizer Downs Zero Plane." *The Bemidji Daily Pioneer*, March 3, 1944.

[52] Uncredited. "Details Received on Death of Lieut. Lizer." *The Bemidji Pioneer*, June 15, 1944.

[53] Uncredited. *Society News. The Bemidji Daily Pioneer*, November 7, 1943.

[54] Uncredited, *The Northern Student*, June 7, 1944.

[55] Uncredited, *The Northern Student*, January 27, 1943.

[56] Seymour, Gideon. "U.S. Not Safe from War." *The Northern Student*, Vol. XV, October 27, 1941.

[57] Shock, John. Letter to Professor Sauer. *The Northern Student*, April 13, 1943.

[58] Uncredited. "Lt. John Shock's Death Reported." *The Northern Student*, October 20, 1944.

[59] Erskine, G. B. Letter to the Parents of John Shock. *The Northern Student*, October 20, 1944.

[60] Uncredited. "For Those Who Gave Their All… Eight Gold Stars." *The Northern Student*, October 20, 1944.

[61] Uncredited. "Former BSTC Athlete Killed Over Burma." *Bemidji Sentinel*, November 24, 1944.

[62] Hobson, D. V. "Credits for Returning Veterans." *The Northern Student*, November 22, 1944.

1945

[63] Uncredited. *The Bemidji Daily Pioneer*, October 15, 1942.

[64] Frazer, James. *The Northern Student*, October 27, 1942.

[65] Uncredited. *The Bemidji Daily Pioneer*, February 16, 1945.

[66] Uncredited. "*Ommaney Bay* (CVE-79)." Naval History and Heritage Command. Accessed July 28, 2021. https://www.history.navy.mil/research/histories/ship-histories/danfs/o/ommaney_bay.html.

[67] Uncredited. "USS *Ommaney Bay* (CVE-79). WreckSite. Accessed July 28, 2021. https://www.wrecksite.eu/wreck.aspx?59770.

[68] Uncredited. *The Northern Student*, January 31, 1945.

[69] Stowell, Donald. *The Northern Student*, February 28, 1945.

[70] Uncredited. "T-5 Donald Jones Killed in Philippines." *The Northern Student*, April 25, 1945.

[71] Dahl, M. Letter to R. H. Jones. *The Northern Student*, May 4, 1945.

[72] Uncredited. *What Goes Alumni? The Northern Student*, April 25, 1945.

[73] Uncredited. *The Northern Student*, April 15, 1945.

[74] Uncredited. *The Bemidji Daily Pioneer*, August 10, 1942.

75 Burkett, Prentiss. *The Unofficial History of the 499ᵗʰ Group.* Temple City, California: Historical Aviation Album, 1981.

76 Conner, Bill. Letter to *The Northern Student. The Northern Student*, June 6, 1945.

77 Nies, Laverne. Letter to *The Northern Student. The Northern Student,* June 6, 1945.

78 Uncredited. *The Northern Student*, June 6, 1945.

REFERENCES

- American Battle Monuments Commission. https://www.abmc.gov/Manila
- https://ccvetmemorial.org/edgar-penford-arnold/
- The Ashkabewis. Project Media. National Indian Education. Minneapolis, Minnesota.
- 340th Engineers in the Pacific by United States Army, Engineer Battalion 340th, 1946. https://archive.org/details/340thEngineersInThePacific/page/n5/mode/2up
- Van Eyck, Manuel F. *Silent Heroes*. Paducah, Kentucky: Turner Publishing, 1990. (ISBN 9781563118067)
- www.Fold3.com
- Wings, Tracks Guns 2019 http://wingstracks-guns.com/dt_gallery/curtiss-p-40-warhawk/curtiss-p-40n-warhawk-sue-42-104589-edit-edit/
- Special Aircraft Service (P-40N Warhawk w/ Chinese National Air Force markings)https://www.sas1946.com/main/index.php?topic=51525.0
- NARA Publication M 1380: *Missing Air Crew Reports (MACRs) of the U.S. Army Air Forces, 1942–1947*, National Archives and Records Administration, Washington. DC, 2005
- Miranda, Justo. *Enemy at the Gates: Panic Fighter of the Second World War*. London: Fonthill Media, 2002. (ISBN 1781557667)
- Hata, Ikuhiko, Yasutto Izawa, and Christopher Shores. *Japanese Army Fighter Aces 1931–1945*. Mechanicsburg, Pennsylvania: Stackpole Books, 2002. (ISBN 9780811710763)
- www.pacificwrecks.com

- WRECK site. https://www.wrecksite.eu/Wrecksite.aspx
- California Militia and National Guard Histories. 40th Infantry Division. http://www.militarymuseum.org/division.html
- Historic Dog Tags. US Army. World War Two. http://www.historicdogtags.com/world-war-24.html
- Bell, Howard, and Anthony Strotman. *The Burma Bridge Busters.* BookSurge, LLC, 2005. (ISBN 1-4196-1555-6)
- Woods, Wiley. *Legacy of the 90th Bombardment Group "The Jolly Rogers."* Paducah, Kentucky: Turner Publishing Company, 1994. ISBN: 1-56311-151-9.
- Vesely, James M. *Unlike Any Land You Know. The story of the "Burma Bridge Busters!" The 490th Bomb Squadron in China-Burma-India.* Writer Club Press, 2000. (ISBN: 0-595-09699-9)

ABOUT THE AUTHOR

DR. MICHAEL HERBERT IS A professor of criminal justice at Bemidji State University, Minnesota. Prior to becoming a professor, Michael spent twenty-three years as a Minnesota peace officer, ten of those years as a SWAT team leader. This is his first book. He lives in northern Minnesota with his wife of thirty-eight years, Deborah. Michael is an amateur WWII Historian and enjoys restoring and collecting WWII vehicles.